The Big Book of Fabulous Fun-Filled Celebrations and Holiday Crafts

The Big Book of Fabulous Fun-Filled Celebrations and Holiday Crafts

BY JIM FOBEL AND JIM BOLEACH

with Virginie Elbert

A Gladstone Book
Holt, Rinehart and Winston
New York

The projects in this book designed by Jim Boleach and Jim Fobel were, except for the food, made by the following people:

Thomas Burgio
Louise Fischer
Arhlene Flowers
Nohad Genadry
Susan Harris
Gail Price
John P. Romer
Lenore Silver
James Silvester
Linda Slocum

All food projects were created and executed by Jim Fobel.

Copyright © 1978 by Gladstone Books, Inc.
All rights reserved, including the right to reproduce
this book or portions thereof in any form.

Published simultaneously in Canada by Holt, Rinehart
and Winston of Canada, Limited.

Library of Congress Cataloging in Publication Data

Fobel, Jim.
   The big book of fabulous, fun-filled celebrations
and holiday crafts.

   "A Gladstone book."
   1. Handicraft. 2. Cookery. 3. Holidays.
I. Boleach, Jim, joint author. II. Title.
TT157.F588 1978   745.59′41   78-4698
ISBN 0-03-040446-0

First Edition

Designer: Allan Mogel
Printed in the United States of America

10 9 8 7 6 5 4 3 2 1

For our friendly family of cats over the years:
Big Cat
Dutchess
Jake
Penelope
Miss Isima
Dorian Grey
Sissy Goforth
Violet
Iris
Charlie
Christopher
Klini
Fritz
McIntosh
Pippin

GENERAL INFORMATION

All materials used in the projects are available at art stores, craft shops, department stores, variety stores, and hardware stores or by mail order, depending on the materials needed.

Patterns can be enlarged by photostatting or by the grid method. If you are using the grid method, follow the steps below to make an enlarged pattern quickly, easily, and accurately.

1. To begin, number the boxes of the grid over the pattern in the book from top to bottom along one side and from left to right along the bottom edge.
2. Then, on whatever you are using to enlarge the pattern—tracing paper, typewriter paper, etc.—draw a grid with 1-inch squares that has the same number of boxes as the grid in the book. Number the squares on the grid you've just drawn as you did on the one in the book.
3. Working square by square with a pencil, duplicate the design in each square of the smaller grid in the corresponding square of the 1-inch grid. Check to make sure that you've drawn all the lines in the correct squares and have crossed the grid lines at the correct angles. Then trace over your pencil lines with a black marking pen. You now have a finished working pattern.

1

New Year's Eve

No matter which calendar is used, or which country is celebrating, New Year's Eve is a joyous time. It's a time for saying good-by to the old year, with its memories of good times and bad, and a time for toasting the unknown year to come, a time for remembering old friends and making new ones. In the Roman days, it was part of the week-long Saturnalia—the unnumbered days at the end of their year of even months.

The gaily decorated replica of a French gas balloon, carrying its cargo of iced champagne, will help you begin your voyage into the New Year in an effervescent mood. The tablecloth and napkins, with their design of colored serpentine and confetti, anticipate the burst of energy and joy you're sure to feel at the stroke of midnight. And the elegant hors d'oeuvres will keep you and your guests happily occupied until it's time to sing *Auld Lang Syne*.

CONFETTI TABLECLOTH AND NAPKINS

Our tablecloth was made to measure 72 inches square to fit up to a 4-foot-square table. You can adjust this measurement to fit your table when you are cutting out the sheet. If you have a round table, make a compass from a piece of string and a pencil and use it to draw the circumference of your table on the sheet; don't forget to allow for some overlap before cutting it out. If you have a very large round table, you may need to start with two sheets stitched together.

Tools and Materials

1 flat, double-size, no-iron bed sheet, in white
ruler
scissors
straight pins
cotton thread, in white
needle or sewing machine
plastic dry-cleaning bag
newspapers
Letraset Pantone markers (permanent ink) with ¼-inch chisel nib:
    one each in cerise, orange, chrome yellow, apple green, turquoise,
    and pink
iron

Instructions

1. Spread the sheet flat over a working surface. Measure and cut out a 74½-inch square for the tablecloth. This allows for a 1-inch-deep hem all around with a ¼-inch-deep turn-under. Also measure and cut out four napkins, each 15¼ inches square. This allows for a ½-inch-deep hem all around with a ¼-inch-deep turn-under.

2. Fold over all hems, pin into place, and stitch either by hand or machine; press in the hems.

3. Split open the plastic bag and spread it over the working surface. Cover with several thicknesses of newspaper to absorb the marking-pen ink, which will go directly through the fabric. Be ready to change newspapers if needed.

4. Experiment with the markers on a leftover piece of sheet to get the "feel" of the colors and the widths of the lines resulting after the ink has spread on the fabric.

5. Cover the tablecloth with serpentine lines of various colors and widths to suggest streamers and with clusters of squares that suggest confetti. Allow for the ink-spreading tendency in planning the pattern. Don't overdo the design by filling in all the white areas—let the individual colors stand out. Make it a joyous, tumbling pattern of streamers and confetti.

6. Repeat on all four napkins, varying the design on each one but condensing the pattern and narrowing the width of the streamers.

7. If necessary, press the finished pieces.

BALLOON CHAMPAGNE BUCKET

Tools and Materials

plastic bucket, 8 inches in top diameter and approximately 10 inches deep

needle-nose pliers

masking tape

ruler

hacksaw

2 aluminum bars, each ⅛ inch thick × ¾ inch wide × 72 inches long

metal file

1 can (2 ounces) PC-7 epoxy paste

tube of cold solder

beach ball, approximately 11 inches in diameter

1 piece sash cable, 8 feet long

3 spray cans (6 ounces each) Blair matte-finish instant color: 2 cans in pineapple and one in orange peel

2 spray cans (4¾ ounces each) Blair clear gloss finish

1 yard satin, in gold

6 yards satin ribbon, 1½ inches wide, in red

scissors

string

white glue

23 yards satin ribbon, ⅞ inch wide: approximately 2 yards in pink, 2 yards in yellow, 6 yards in light green, 6 yards in light blue, and 7 yards in red

plastic container to just fit inside bucket, in white

Instructions

1. Remove bucket handle with pliers. Bend the two handle flaps to the inside of the bucket and hold them in place with masking tape. (When supports are put into position, two of the supports will press against the flaps and hold them in position.)

2. With the hacksaw, cut four lengths from the aluminum bars, each 26 inches long. File the cut ends smooth. One inch down from one end of each bar, which will become the top end, cut a ⅜-inch-long slot into the width of each bar that is just wide enough to accommodate the sash cable, as shown in the diagram. Also file a groove into

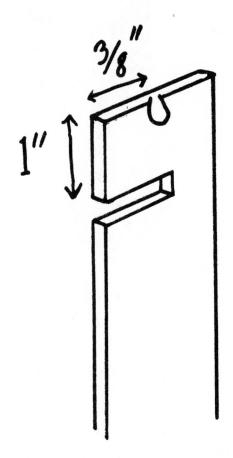

part of the thickness of the top of each bar just above the inside end of the cut, as shown.

3. Place the four bars inside the bucket, top ends up and grooves facing out. Place one of them over each taped-down bucket flap and the other two exactly between. Following manufacturer's directions for mixing and using PC-7 epoxy paste, attach the support bars to the inner wall of the bucket. When the epoxy is dry, fill in the immediate area between the sides of the bars and the bucket wall with cold solder, smoothing the narrow joint.

4. Wrap the center portion of the sash cable once around the beach ball at the seam line and twist the ends once around each other at the meeting point. Then, bring the ends up and over the other half of the ball—just as though you were tying up a box with string. When the

ends of the cable are back at the joining point, make two loops around the joint and twist the ends to make a firm closing. Cut off the extra sash cable, and tuck in the ends.

5. Spray the beach ball with the pineapple yellow paint. If you need two coats, let the paint dry between applications. Spray the bucket with the orange peel color. Let dry. Then spray both with clear gloss. Let dry very thoroughly before proceeding to the next step.

6. Now attach the ball to the supports. Fit the sash cable into the slots on the four supports, as shown in the diagram. Turn the ball so that

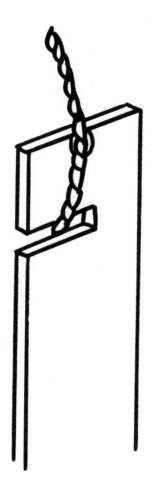

you can hook the two points at which the cables intersect into opposite supports—one part of the cable should now support the ball from below. For even more support, put a little epoxy paste between each support and the sash cable.

7. Wind ⅞-inch-wide red, light green, and blue ribbon around the supports barber-pole fashion, alternating the colors along the length. Tape or glue the top ends to the top of the support posts and the bottom ends inside the bucket edge. Starting behind one support top, glue a length of each color ribbon over the top half of the ball, ending it behind the opposite support. Repeat to add ribbon in the other direction.

8. Using the gold satin, piece together a strip that is about 10 inches wide and 2½ yards long; join the short ends. Then double the strip so that the raw edges are on the inside of the circle, as shown in the diagram. With raw edges against the ball, loop the swag between

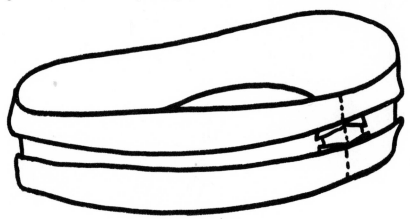

each two supports so that it hangs against the ball in four graceful curves. Tie the swag at each support post with a piece of string.

9. Cut the red 1½-inch-wide ribbon into eight equal lengths. Following the diagrams, make four bows and attach them to the gold-ribbon

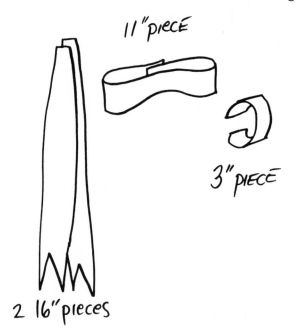

11" piece

3" piece

2 16" pieces

swag at the top of each support with white glue or masking tape.

10. Next cut four lengths of each of the ⅞-inch-wide ribbons as follows:

 red: 10-inch lengths
 pink: 12-inch lengths
 yellow: 13-inch lengths
 light green: 15-inch lengths
 light blue: 17-inch lengths
 red: 19-inch lengths

Following the order of ribbon colors, with the 10-inch ribbon at the top, make a swag of ribbons around the bucket between each two supports. Tape each end to the support where it joins the top of the bucket.

11. Cover the base area of the supports where the swag ends and the pole-wrapping ends meet by cutting four 4-inch-long pieces of pink

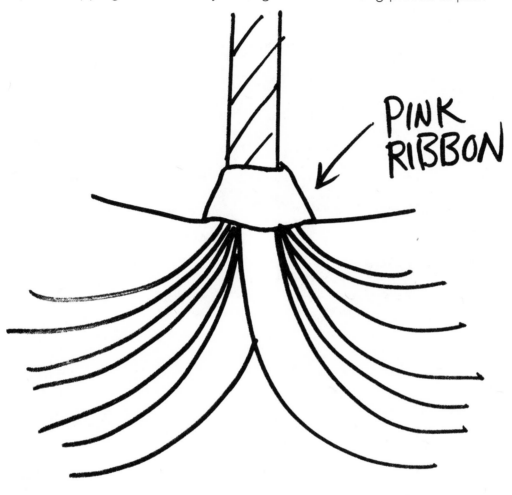

PINK RIBBON

ribbon and wrapping each around one of these areas, holding it in position with white glue.

12. The final step is to place the white plastic container inside the decorated bucket. The container not only hides the inner construction but waterproofs the bucket as well.

ELEGANT HORS D'OEUVRES:

Breast of Chicken with Asparagus Tips
Roast Beef with Sweet Gherkins
Cornets of Ham with Egg Filling
Roast Pork with Pineapple
Pâté with Sautéed Mushrooms

To make our delicious glazed hors d'oeuvres, have the man at your local delicatessen cut the meat needed into the sizes specified below or do it yourself at home. Our hors d'oeuvres are rather large so they must be served on plates with knives and forks. If you wish to make them smaller, cut the meat slices in half before beginning (except the ham–use smaller squares if you wish the cornets to be smaller) and use only one garnish on each. Arrange all meat slices on dinner plates or cookie sheets and refrigerate them until you are ready to assemble the hors d'oeuvres. Since these hors d'oeuvres take several hours to prepare, you might want to make them the day before the party and refrigerate them overnight. Makes 20 large hors d'oeuvres.

Tools and Materials

4 slices (2 ounces each) roast breast of chicken (each 3 to 4 inches long)
4 slices (2 ounces each) roast beef (each 3 to 4 inches long)
4 slices (2 ounces each) roast pork (each 3 to 4 inches long)
4 slices (2 ounces each) pâté (homemade, canned, or purchased fresh) (each 3 to 4 inches long)
4 slices boiled ham, each 4 inches square
Aspic (recipe follows)
Egg Filling (recipe follows)
8 canned or fresh asparagus tips
8 small sweet gherkins

Wooden Reindeer Table

Pressed Flower Card and Gift Wrap

Collage Gift Box and Card

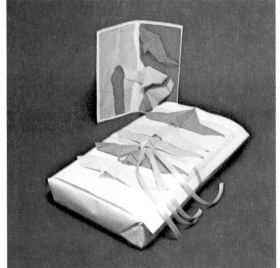

Origami Cards

Chinese Lantern

A Contemporary Wooden Menorah

20

Shrimp Christmas Tree

Elegant Hors d'Oeuvres

Dragon Mask Cake

21

Bird's-Nest Tree Ornaments

A Christmas Box Train

23

Block-Printed Star of David Wrapping Paper

Balloon Champagne Bucket

2 cucumber slices with peel
2 unpitted black olives
4 chunks fresh or canned pineapple
12 slices fresh or canned mushrooms
kitchen sieve
pastry bag with #30 star tip
kitchen shears
cheesecloth or linen napkin

1. Make the Aspic:

ASPIC
2 cans (13 ounces each) or 3¼ cups homemade chicken broth
½ cup dry white wine
2 envelopes (2 tablespoons) unflavored gelatin
3 tablespoons diced onion
2 eggs
1 tablespoon vinegar
1 bay leaf
salt and pepper to taste

Combine the broth, wine, gelatin, and onion in a saucepan over medium heat. Separate the egg whites from the yolks and reserve the yolks for another use. Crush the egg shells and add them to the pan along with the egg whites (the crushed shells and whites will clarify the aspic when it is strained). Add the vinegar, bay leaf, and salt and pepper to taste. Bring to a boil, stirring constantly, over medium heat. Reduce the heat to very low so that the mixture barely simmers and cook, without stirring, for 15 minutes. Moisten the cheesecloth or linen napkin and wring it out. If using cheesecloth, place a double layer into the sieve; if using a linen napkin, line the sieve with one layer. Ladle the aspic through the cloth-lined sieve into a bowl. Let the aspic chill slightly in the refrigerator, stirring occasionally, until it begins to set. The aspic should be the consistency of heavy syrup when ready to use. If your aspic "sets" because it has chilled too long, simply place it in a small pan over low heat until it melts slightly and then refrigerate it again until it is the consistency of heavy syrup.

2. Prepare the garnishes. If using fresh asparagus, steam the tips in a small amount of water until tender but still firm; drain them on paper towels. Drain the gherkins and dry on paper towels. Cut the cucumber slices in half and remove the centers. Cut four small slices from one unpitted black olive for the ham cornets and cut four small diamonds from the other olive for the tops of the pineapple chunks. Lightly brown the mushroom slices in a small amount of butter and drain on paper towels.

3. Make the cornets of ham.

EGG FILLING
7 hard-cooked egg yolks
4 tablespoons (½ stick) butter, at room temperature
2 tablespoons mayonnaise
1 teaspoon dried mustard (optional)
salt and pepper to taste

Rub the egg yolks through a fine sieve into a bowl. Add the remaining ingredients and stir with a fork to make a smooth consistency. If too stiff, add additional mayonnaise to make a smooth consistency. Spoon into the pastry bag. To make each cornet, lay a slice of ham on your work surface and shape into a cone. With the cornet in your left hand, trim away excess ham to make the top edge even. With cornet remaining in left hand, fill with egg mixture, using a circular motion as you reach the top, as shown. Lay the cornet onto a plate, seam side down, when you finish it. Make three more cornets in this way. Place a black olive slice in the center of the egg filling of each cornet and refrigerate them until ready to glaze.

4. Each hors d'oeuvre will be glazed twice. For the first glazing, simply spoon a tablespoonful of the syrupy aspic over each slice of meat and over each ham cornet, taking care not to let the aspic run over the egg filling in the cornets; smooth the aspic with the back of a spoon. Chill the glazed meats until the aspic has completely set.

5. To attach the garnishes, dip each in aspic and arrange as follows: Place two asparagus tips on each slice of chicken, two gherkins on each slice of roast beef, one-half slice of cucumber on each ham cornet, one pineapple chunk topped with an olive diamond on each slice of roast pork, and three slices of mushroom slightly overlapping each other on each slice of pâté. Chill until the aspic has set.

6. For the final glazing, spoon a tablespoon of aspic (remember that the consistency should still be that of heavy syrup) over each, making sure that it is evenly distributed. Chill all hors d'oeuvres until aspic has set. The hors d'oeuvres may be loosely covered with aluminum foil and refrigerated for one day, until ready to arrange on a tray. To arrange, use a sharp, pointed knife to cut around each hors d'oeuvre, thus trimming away any excess aspic that may have accumulated, and transfer them with a spatula to a serving tray. Remember: Cold hors d'oeuvres should be served cold. *Makes 20 large hors d'oeuvres.*

2

Chinese New Year

The Chinese New Year is a celebration that takes place between the end of January and the middle of February, starting on the day of the new moon and lasting for fourteen days, until the full moon. To celebrate it, cloth dragon shapes are draped over the heads and shoulders of marchers who dance through the streets. Shopkeepers stuff the dragons' open mouths with heads of lettuce as an offering to the New Year, and the air is filled with the sounds of music and bursting firecrackers, and feasting is almost constant. On the fourteenth night, under the full moon, the most sacred ceremony of all takes place—the Feast of Lanterns, when everyone vies to create the most unusual lantern to hang outside the door or on a tree or pole. This custom honors an ancient emperor who had large lanterns made to float in the sky on this night of the full moon's light. Our lantern, lighted with tiny Christmas tree lights, presides over the Chinese feast, which ends with a gloriously decorated Dragon Mask Cake, with its curly orange and turquoise frosting and gleaming silver teeth.

CHINESE LANTERN

To light our lantern, we've added a string of tiny Christmas tree lights to the inside. If you wish to light your lantern, be sure to spray the wood and rice paper with fireproofing first.

Tools and Materials

#1 X-acto knife with #11 blades
6 balsa wood dowels, ¼ × ½ inch, each 3 feet long
7 balsa wood dowels, ¼ × ¼ inch, each 3 feet long
ruler
pencil
white glue
artist's fine-pointed paintbrush (for glue)
4 cork balls with small hole partway through center, each ⅞ inch in
    diameter (available at craft-supply and fishing-supply stores)
tracing paper, at least 9 × 12 inches
lightweight cardboard
masking tape
1 sheet illustration board, 20 × 30 inches, in white
2 sheets rice paper, each 25 × 37 inches: one sheet in ochre and one
    in Moriki white
small, flat wooden stick
1 spool (1 ounce) copper wire, #26-gauge
20 teardrop-shaped stone beads, each ⅞ inch long

Instructions

1. Using the X-acto knife, cut the doweling into the lengths specified on the diagrams to make five boxes, one in each of the following sizes:

Box A: 3 inches long by 3 inches wide by 2 inches deep, using ¼- by ¼-inch doweling

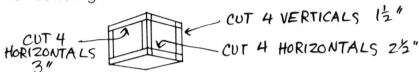

CUT 4 HORIZONTALS 3"

CUT 4 VERTICALS 1½"

CUT 4 HORIZONTALS 2½"

Box B: 4 inches long by 4 inches wide by 2½ inches deep, using ¼- by ¼-inch doweling

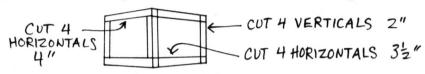

CUT 4 HORIZONTALS 4"

CUT 4 VERTICALS 2"

CUT 4 HORIZONTALS 3½"

Box C: 5 inches long by 5 inches wide by 3 inches deep, using ¼- by ¼-inch doweling

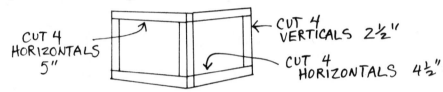

CUT 4 HORIZONTALS 5"

CUT 4 VERTICALS 2½"

CUT 4 HORIZONTALS 4½"

Box D: 6 inches long by 6 inches wide by 3 inches deep, using ¼- by ¼-inch doweling for the vertical side pieces and ¼- by ½-inch doweling for the horizontal strips

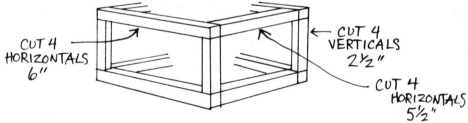

CUT 4 HORIZONTALS 6"

CUT 4 VERTICALS 2½"

CUT 4 HORIZONTALS 5½"

Box E: 8 inches long by 8 inches wide by 4 inches deep, using ¼- by ¼-inch doweling for the vertical side pieces and ¼- by ½-inch doweling for the horizontal strips

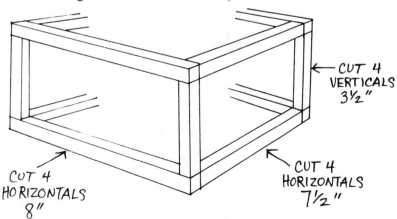

CUT 4 HORIZONTALS 8"

CUT 4 VERTICALS 3½"

CUT 4 HORIZONTALS 7½"

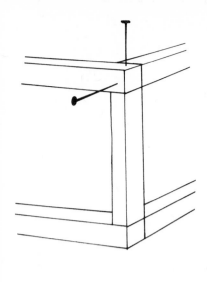

2. Glue the doweling pieces together to make the five boxes specified in step 1. Hold each joint in place with two straight pins inserted as shown in the diagram.

3. Brace Box E as follows: Using the ¼- by ¼-inch doweling, cut two lengths, each 10¾ inches long. Following the diagram, cut a point on each end of each piece. Then glue one length diagonally across the bottom of the box, fitting the pointed ends into opposite corners. When the glue has dried, glue the other length across the other diagonal, positioning it on top of the first piece, as shown.

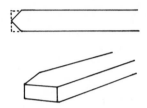

ANGLE BRACE PATTERN ACTUAL SIZE

4. Add four cork-ball feet to the bottom of Box E. Push a straight pin through the center of each cork ball. Brush glue on each corner of the bottom of the box and push the ball with the pin into the wood of each corner.

5. Trace the brace pattern on tracing paper, glue it to a piece of cardboard, and cut it out. Lay the pattern on a length of ¼- by ¼-inch doweling, trace around it, and cut it out with the X-acto knife. Trace and cut twenty-three more in the same way. These braces will hold

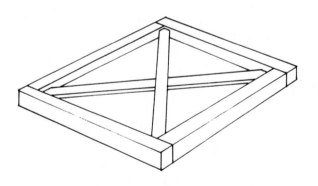

the boxes together, one above the other, and also form the support rafters for the slanting roofs to be added later. There will be two braces on each side between Boxes E and D and between Boxes D and C; one brace will be on each side between Boxes C and B and between Box B and A. Fit the braces in position, following the diagram for placement, and scrape off any bits of wood that may be in the way. Glue the braces in position and hold them in place with masking tape. Remove the tape when the glue is dry.

6. Trace the corner brace pattern on tracing paper, glue it to a piece of cardboard, and cut it out. Lay the pattern on a piece of ¼-by ¼-inch doweling, trace around it, and cut it out with the X-acto knife. Cut fifteen more in the same way. Following the diagram, glue each in place, holding them with masking tape. When the glue is dry, remove the tape.

CORNER BRACE PATTERN ACTUAL SIZE

30

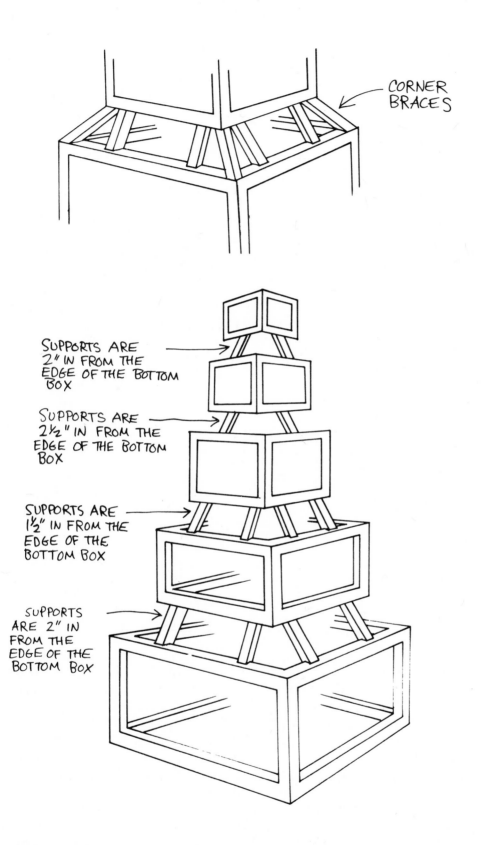

CORNER BRACES

SUPPORTS ARE 2" IN FROM THE EDGE OF THE BOTTOM BOX

SUPPORTS ARE 2½" IN FROM THE EDGE OF THE BOTTOM BOX

SUPPORTS ARE 1½" IN FROM THE EDGE OF THE BOTTOM BOX

SUPPORTS ARE 2" IN FROM THE EDGE OF THE BOTTOM BOX

7. Enlarge the roof patterns by the grid method. Lay them on the illustration board and cut them out with the X-acto, holding the X-acto as you would a pencil and drawing the blade toward you as you cut.

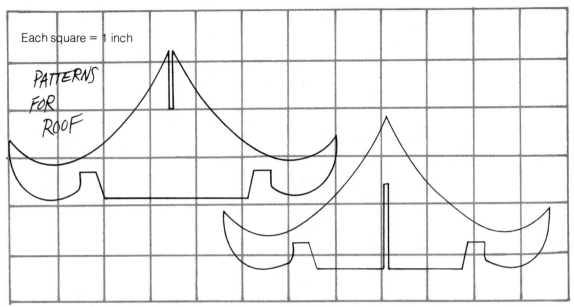

Each square = 1 inch

PATTERNS FOR ROOF

You may have to cut along the lines several times to cut through. To cut neat corners, draw the blade a bit past each intersection. Assemble the two pieces by slipping one notch into the other.

8. Enlarge the roof covering pattern by the grid method. Glue it to

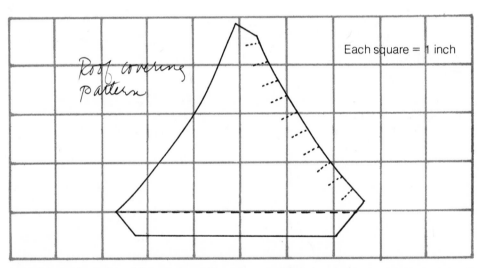

Each square = 1 inch

Roof covering pattern

cardboard and cut it out. Lay it on the ochre rice paper, trace around it, and cut it out. Cut three more in this way. Make a fold on the bottom and the right-hand edge of each piece where the dotted lines on the pattern indicate. Unfold the right-hand edge and make in it several cuts going from the edge of the paper to the fold line. Using the flat, wooden stick, spread a very little glue—too much glue will cause the rice paper to wrinkle—on the right-hand folded edge of one piece. Position the piece so that it covers the area between two of the lantern-top supports, gluing the right-hand edge over the support to the right, as shown in the diagram. On a second piece of roof covering, apply glue to the right-hand folded edge, as above, and along the very edge of the left-hand side. Position the folded, glued edge over the next uncovered lantern-top support and lay the left-hand edge on top of the glued seam made previously. Working your way

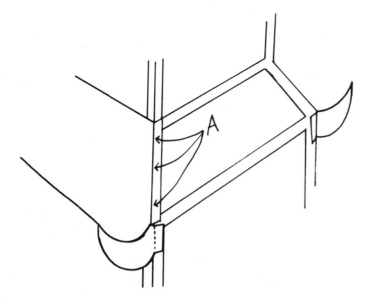

around the supports, add the remaining two pieces of roof covering the same way. Finally, apply glue along the left-hand edge of the first piece you applied and lay it on top of the right-hand edge of the last piece glued.

9. Trace the pattern for the curved roof decorations, glue it to a piece of cardboard, and cut it out. Lay it on the illustration board, trace around it, and cut it out. Cut out fifteen more in the same way. With a straight pin, make a small hole in the place indicated by the dot on the pattern in each piece. Lightly score both sides of each piece where indicated by the dotted line on the pattern. Now, carefully split the thickness of the board up to this scored line, as shown in the diagram. Pull back the split ends, brush each with glue, and press each end in turn against each side of the top of a corner support so that two sides of the dowel are covered. Repeat until all boxes except Box A have corner decorations.

10. Make the patterns for the slanting rooftops: First, roll over a piece of tape and stick it to the left-hand corner roof support of Box E. Allowing ½ inch of paper to extend beyond the left-hand edge, press a piece of tracing paper on top of the tape to hold it in position, as shown. With the X-acto knife, cut the paper along the left-hand edge

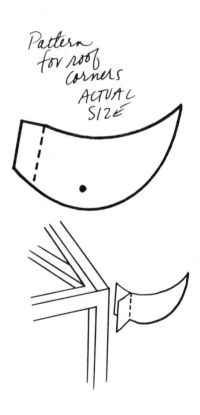

Pattern for roof corners ACTUAL SIZE

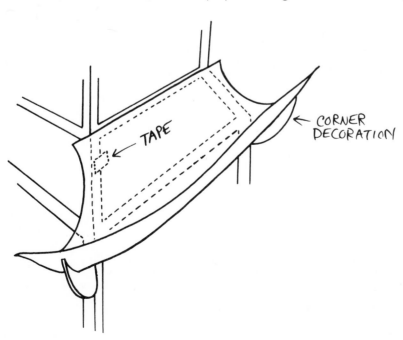

TAPE
← CORNER DECORATION

so that it is flush with the edge of the support and the curved roof decoration, carrying the cut ½ inch beyond the point of the roof decoration. On the right-hand side, cut down in the same way but leave about ¼ inch of paper extending beyond the edge. Next, cut across between the points of the two roof decorations but leave about ½ inch of paper extending beyond the edge. Then cut straight across the top. The pattern is now complete.

11. Remove the roof pattern, but leave the tape in place. Make ¼-inch-deep cuts along the lower, curved edge of the right-hand side, as indicated on the pattern. Check the fit of the pattern around all four sides of the lantern top—if any minor adjustments are necessary, make them while you are cutting the rice paper. Lay the pattern on the ochre rice paper, trace around it, and cut it out. Repeat three more times. Fold under the ½-inch margin on all four lower roof edges and very lightly glue them to the back of the paper. These will give added weight to the pieces. Make the ¼-inch-deep cuts in the lower half of the right-hand edges of each piece.

12. Press one edge of one piece of roof covering on the tape on the left-hand corner to hold it in place. Always placing the glue on the wood, not the paper, glue the ¼-inch extension, marked A on the diagram, on the right-hand side over the dowel roof support. Add the next roof section in the same way, bringing the ¼-inch extension, marked B on the diagram, of the first section glued over the B part of the second section; glue down. Also add a line of glue to the edge of the illustration-board curved-roof decorations and press the rice paper against the glue. Continue around the four sides in this way, adding all four roof pieces. When you get to the tape, remove it and add a bit of glue in its place; push the left-hand edge of the first piece glued against it. Repeat the pattern making, cutting of ochre rice paper, and gluing down of the roof sections on all the remaining levels.

13. Now cover the sides of the boxes with white rice paper. Cut the following sizes for the separate boxes:

    Box A: 2¼ by 12¼ inches
    Box B: 2½ by 16¼ inches
    Box C: 3 by 20¼ inches
    Box D: 3 by 24¼ inches
    Box E: 4 by 32¼ inches

Wrap each strip around the appropriate box, gluing it to each corner dowel as you go. Remember to put the glue only on the wood, not the paper. As you come to each corner, cut a slit in the paper to accommodate the curved roof decorations. Turn the extra ¼ inch under at the final dowel corner before you glue it.

14. Set the lantern top on top of Box A so that the notches fit over the corner supports.

15. The final step is to hang the narrow, teardrop-shaped beads from each corner decoration. Cut twenty 2½-inch-long pieces of copper wire. Thread one length of wire through each bead, pull the ends even, and twist them against the bead to hold it steady. Pass each wire through the hole in the bottom curve of each corner decoration, and twist the wire together to hold it in place.

DRAGON MASK CAKE

Our spectacular dragon mask cake will serve 35 to 40 people.

Tools and Materials

2 sheet-cake pans, each 13 × 9 × 2 inches (if you have only one pan, bake one cake at a time)
3 boxes (approximately 19 ounces each) cake mix, any flavor
electric mixer
stainless steel bowl, 9 inches in diameter
Butter Cream Frosting (recipe follows)
White Frosting (recipe follows)
rectangular serving tray, at least 9 × 13 inches
food coloring, in red, yellow, blue, and green (the paste form will produce the brightest colors)
pastry bag with #30 star tip, #11 round tip (or other plain round tip with 3/16-inch opening), and #68 leaf tip
silver candy dragees, in assorted sizes and shapes (if not available, substitute silver balls, candy corn, Good 'n Plenty, jelly beans, or aluminum foil cut into shapes)
noise makers or other party items with frilly crepe-paper ends
2 party toothpicks with cellophane frills.

Instructions

1. Preheat oven to temperature specified on cake-mix box. Generously grease and lightly flour the two cake pans.

2. Prepare two boxes of the cake mix in a large mixing bowl, following package directions. Divide the batter evenly between the two pans. Tap the pans up and down on a counter several times until all air bubbles come to the surface (this will help to ensure that the cakes will rise evenly). Bake the cakes on separate racks in the oven for 35 to 40 minutes, or until a toothpick inserted in the centers comes out clean and dry. Cool cakes in the pans for 10 minutes and then turn out onto racks to cool. Do not turn oven off.

3. Generously grease and lightly flour the stainless steel bowl. Prepare the third cake mix, following package directions, and pour into the prepared bowl. Again, tap it up and down several times to help air bubbles rise to the surface. Bake for 1 hour to 1 hour and 15 minutes, or until it tests done with a toothpick (this cake takes longer to bake because it is a deeper one). Cool for 10 minutes in the bowl and then turn out onto a rack to cool. Let all cakes cool thoroughly before proceeding.

4. Prepare the Butter Cream Frosting:

BUTTER CREAM FROSTING

1 pound butter, at room temperature
½ cup solid white shortening
3 pounds confectioners sugar
1 cup milk
almond, lemon, orange, or peppermint extract to taste (optional)

Cream the butter and shortening together in a large mixing bowl with an electric mixer at medium speed for 3 minutes, scraping the sides of the bowl occasionally with a rubber spatula. Add ½ cup of the confectioners sugar, beating until it is thoroughly incorporated. Continue to add the confectioners sugar ½ cup at a time, blending it in thoroughly before each addition. When the icing becomes too stiff to beat, add 1 tablespoon of milk and blend it in. Continue adding 1 tablespoon of milk and small amounts of confectioners sugar at a time as you continue to beat until all is used up. Add extract to taste if you wish. If frosting is too stiff, beat in a small amount of milk. This procedure will result in an extra light and fluffy butter cream icing. Set aside but do not refrigerate or frosting will set. *Makes 9 cups.*

5. Prepare the White Frosting:

WHITE FROSTING

½ cup solid white shortening
1 pound confectioners sugar
3 to 4 tablespoons milk

Cream shortening for 3 minutes in a medium mixing bowl at medium speed with an electric mixer, scraping the sides of the bowl with a spatula occasionally. Begin adding sugar ½ cup at a time as you continue to beat until most of the sugar has been added and the frosting is stiff. Begin adding milk, a drop or two at a time, alternately with the sugar until both are used up, still continuing to beat. Set aside but do not refrigerate or frosting will set. *Makes 3 cups.*

6. Place one of the rectangular cakes, flattest side up, on a serving

tray. Spread top with a thin layer of Butter Cream Frosting and place second rectangular cake, flattest side down, over the frosted layer.
7. Spread a 9-inch circle—approximately ¼ inch in depth—of Butter Cream Frosting at one end of the top rectangular cake and invert the bowl-shaped cake over the frosting, as shown in the illustration.

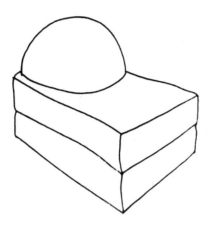

Using a long, sharp knife, trim away the four squared corners of the cake, as shown in the illustration.

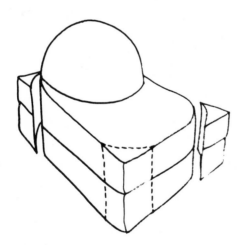

8. Using a small spatula and the White Frosting, thinly frost the front half of the bowl-shaped cake (this will become the white part of the eyes). Tint 1 cup White Frosting with three drops red food coloring to make pink. Using a spatula, thinly frost the area where the mouth will be, as shown in the illustration.

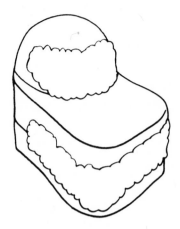

9. Tint 1 cup of White Frosting with enough blue food coloring to make a royal blue color. Fit the #30 star tip into the pastry bag and fill it with the blue icing. Outline the tops of the eyes and then the bottoms, making them so that they almost touch in the center, as shown.

Onto the two nostril areas of the dragon, squeeze out two oval shapes, using the same blue frosting, as shown in the illustration.

Then squeeze out a series of five elongated U shapes, one on top of another and each getting progressively smaller, over the two blue ovals, as shown.

Squeeze out three whisker shapes at the front center of the dragon, below where his mouth will go. Clean the pastry bag, drying it thoroughly, and fit it with the leaf tip.

10. Tint approximately 1 cup of the Butter Cream Frosting with 3 drops yellow food coloring to make a pastel shade of yellow; fill prepared pastry bag. Beginning at the center front, between the eyes, squeeze out a series of overlapping leaves to outline the eyes, as shown.

Clean out the pastry bag, drying it thoroughly, and fit it with the #11 plain tip.

11. Tint the remaining White Frosting combined with 1 cup of Butter Cream Frosting with 5 drops of blue and ½ drop yellow food coloring and blend thoroughly to achieve a pale turquoise frosting. (If you wish a darker color, add additional color.) Beginning near the front between the eyes, squeeze out balls of frosting. To do this, hold the tip in one place as you squeeze and then move it closer to the cake as you stop squeezing. Squeeze out balls of icing until the entire top of the head is covered. Clean out the pastry bag, dry it thoroughly, and refit it with the #11 plain tip.

12. Tint 1 cup of Butter Cream Frosting with enough red food coloring to make a bright red; fill the prepared bag. Squeeze out a ball of red into the center of each nostril. Outline the mouth with red, as shown in the illustration. Squeeze out several short lines of red behind the eyes.

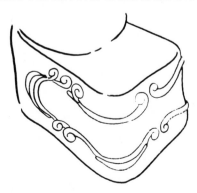

Clean and dry the pastry bag and refit it with the #11 plain tip.

13. Tint the remaining Butter Cream Frosting with enough equal parts of red and yellow food coloring to make an orange frosting. Fill the bag with orange frosting and squeeze out balls of orange in all areas where there is no frosting. Note that you can make large or small balls by the amount of pressure you apply as you squeeze. Make small balls when you need to fill in a small area and large balls to fill in larger areas. Clean out the bag, dry it, and fit it with the plain tip.

14. To make the eyeballs, tint a small amount of any leftover colored frosting with red, blue, and green coloring to make a black color; fill the prepared bag. Beginning at the center of the eye and working outwards, make a spiral of color to form the pupil of the eye.

15. Insert a silver dragee into each turquoise ball and into each orange ball between the nostrils. Also press in silver dragees for teeth all around the inside of the mouth shape.

16. Insert a frilly party toothpick into the center of each nostril. Attach several "party" frills—from noise makers, etc.—to the back of the dragon mask by inserting them through the icing at the back of the mask.

17. If your refrigerator is large enough, refrigerate the cake until the frosting has set; otherwise store it in a cool place until serving time. *Serves 35 to 40.*

3

St. Valentine's Day

St. Valentine's Day means hearts and lace and flowers—lovers' gifts and sentiments. According to the popular version, Valentine's Day had its simple beginning in the third century when St. Valentine, a Roman martyr, died on February 14th in a prison cell, leaving a last message to his jailer's young daughter. The message was signed "from your Valentine." The day has acquired symbols and decorations along the way—the cupids from mythology, the clasped hands so beloved by the Victorian world, lace paper decorations of the Victorian and Edwardian cards, the hothouse flowers and roses to match red hearts.

If you find Valentine's Day too fleeting, try our baker's-clay valentine that can be hung on the kitchen wall to be cherished all year through. A heart-shaped pie, its fluted edge mimicking a lace edging, and with a center of shining, luscious cherries topped with a pastry heart, is a perfect gift for a favorite person. The traditionally red sachet heart with its ruffled embroidered edge is filled with the spicy, sweet scent of summer flowers and is classically accompanied by one tiny sweetheart rose.

A POTPOURRI HEART

Place this sweet-smelling heart in a drawer to scent scarves or lingerie, add a loop of narrow red ribbon and hang it in a closet to fragrance clothes, or wear it around your neck on a piece of red velvet or satin.

Tools and Materials

pencil
1 sheet tracing paper, 8½ × 11 inches
scissors
1 piece fabric, 5 × 11 inches, in red
straight pins
sewing thread, in red and white
needle or sewing machine
potpourri
1 yard embroidered eyelet, 1½ inches wide, in white

Instructions

1. Using the pencil on the tracing paper, trace the heart pattern. Cut it out.
2. Fold the fabric in half, right sides together, so that it measures 5½ by 5 inches. Pin the heart pattern to the fabric and cut out two hearts at one time.
3. Pin the hearts together, right sides together, sew around the edge, making a ⅜-inch-deep seam. Leave a 2-inch opening from the point of the heart up one side. Turn the heart right side out through the opening.

HEART PATTERN
ACTUAL SIZE

4. Fill the heart with enough potpourri to make a nice, plump heart.

5. Sew up the opening, using a blind stitch.

6. To make a ruffle, run small stitches along the straight edge of the eyelet. Remove the needle and pull on the loose end of the thread, ruffling the material slightly. (You may only need 30 inches instead of 36 inches but do not cut off the excess until the ruffle is pinned around the edge of the heart.) Starting at the point of the heart, pin the ruffle all along the seam. Cut off any excess material, and sew the ruffle in place with a blind stitch. Seam the two ends of the ruffle together at the bottom point with a French seam so that the raw edges are hidden.

HEART-SHAPED CHERRY PIE

Makes one 9-inch pie.

Tools and Materials

enough pie crust for a 9-inch, two-crust pie (use a 10-ounce package
    of pie-crust mix or your own recipe)
heart-shaped pan, 9 inches in diameter
pencil
tracing paper, 8½ × 11 inches
scissors
pastry wheel
2 baking sheets
granulated sugar
aluminum foil
3 to 4 cups raw rice or dried beans
3 cups vanilla pudding (use pudding mix or your own recipe)
Cherry Glaze (recipe follows)
1 jar (8 ounces) maraschino cherries or 1 can (16 ounces) tart pie
    cherries, with liquid

44

Instructions

1. Preheat oven to 425 degrees F.

2. In a medium mixing bowl, combine pie-crust ingredients until blended, following package directions if you are using a mix.

3. Roll out half the pastry on a lightly floured surface to a ⅛-inch thickness. Fit it loosely into the heart-shaped pan and trim excess pastry away with a kitchen knife.

4. Using the pencil on the piece of tracing paper, trace the heart pattern. Cut it out.

5. Roll out the remaining pastry and scraps to a ⅛-inch thickness. Lay the heart pattern over the pastry and trace around the edge with a sharp knife or pastry wheel. Place heart on a small, ungreased baking sheet, and sprinkle heart lightly with granulated sugar. Place in refrigerator.

6. Using the pastry wheel, cut the remaining pastry into four 1½-inch-wide strips, each 12 inches long.

7. Moisten with a little water the edge of the pastry in the heart-shaped pan. Beginning at the center of the top of the heart, make the upright ruffled edge. Do this by attaching ½ inch of one long edge of a pastry strip to the moistened edge of the pastry in the pan. Using your fingers, make a pleat in the pastry at this point. Continue to pleat the strip as you work and then press the pleated pastry strip against the moistened pastry to hold it in place. Make sure that all the pleats face in the same direction. Moisten the edge of the pastry with additional water if necessary to hold the pleats in place. When you need to add a second strip of pastry, overlap the end of the first strip slightly to hide the spot where they meet. Continue adding strips in this way until you have made a ruffle all around the edge of the heart-shaped pan.

8. Line the pastry in the pan with a sheet of aluminum foil, working it gently with your fingers to conform to the inside of the pastry. Fill the foil with raw rice or raw dried beans.

9. Place pan on a second baking sheet, and put it in the preheated oven for 8 to 10 minutes, or until the edges are golden and the pastry is firm. The ruffled edge will flatten out so that it forms a frame around the heart.

10. Carefully remove the baking sheet from the oven. Lift out the aluminum foil and rice or beans—protect your fingers with a folded-over towel. (Save the rice or beans in a covered jar for other pastry making.) Return the pastry to the oven for another 4 or 5 minutes to complete baking. Watch carefully during this time to prevent the bottom from puffing up, pricking it with a fork in several places and using a wooden spoon to push the pastry back in shape when necessary. When the pastry bottom is firm, remove the pan from the oven and cool the pie crust in the pan. Do not turn off the oven.

11. Remove the baking sheet holding the small, heart-shaped pastry from the refrigerator. Place it in the oven and bake it for 5 to 8 minutes, or until golden and crisp. Remove and cool.

12. Add 3 cups of your favorite vanilla pudding to the pie crust, almost filling it. Let cool.

13. Prepare the Cherry Glaze:

CHERRY GLAZE

2 tablespoons cornstarch
½ cup liquid drained from cherries
2 tablespoons sugar
2 tablespoons butter
several drops red food coloring

Measure the cornstarch into a small saucepan. Add the cherry juice and stir until blended. Stir in ¼ cup cold water and the sugar and cook over medium heat, stirring constantly, until mixture begins to boil. Remove from the heat and stir in the butter and food coloring.
14. Drain the cherries well on paper towels. If using maraschino cherries, cut them in half. If using tart pie cherries, leave them whole. Arrange the cherries over the pie filling around the outside edge only, as shown in the project photograph, and spoon the glaze over them. Center the small, heart-shaped pastry on top and chill the pie until ready to serve. *Makes one 9-inch pie.*

HEART PATTERN
ACTUAL SIZE

KITCHEN VALENTINE WALL HANGING

Tools and Materials

Baker's Clay (recipe follows)
rolling pin
ruler
kitchen knife
cookie sheet
tracing paper, 8½ × 11 inches
pencil
scissors
1 egg yolk
watercolor brush, #3
red food coloring
straight pin
white glue
1 piece felt, 7 × 10 inches, in red

Instructions

1. Set all materials out before beginning. Prepare the Baker's Clay:

BAKER'S CLAY

4 cups all-purpose flour
1 cup salt
1¼ cups warm water
¼ cup glycerin

In a large mixing bowl, combine the flour and salt until well blended; add the water and glycerin all at once and mix by hand until a stiff

47

dough is formed. Knead the dough on a lightly floured surface for 5 minutes or until it is very smooth. Lightly dust the rolling pin and your work surface with flour, and roll out the dough to a ⅜-inch thickness. Using the ruler and the kitchen knife, cut a 7-by-10-inch rectangle out of the lower right-hand corner of the dough.

2. Place the rectangle on the cookie sheet, taking care not to stretch the dough. Using the pencil and tracing paper, trace the heart pattern

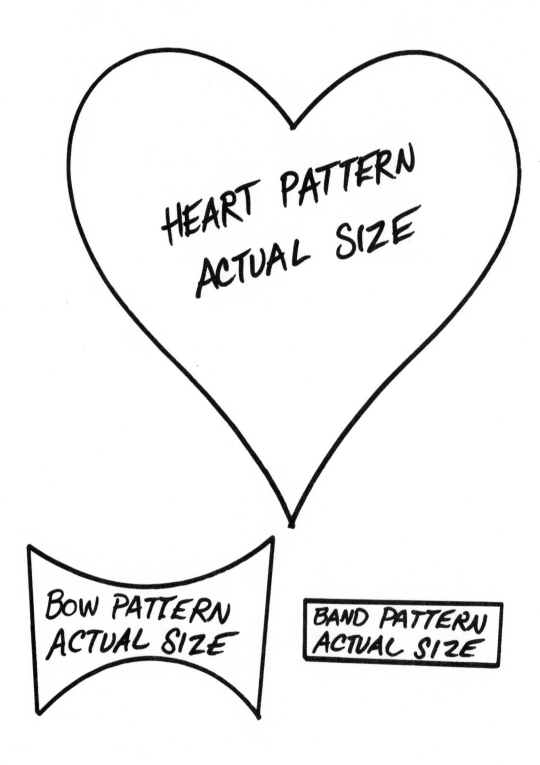

HEART PATTERN ACTUAL SIZE

BOW PATTERN ACTUAL SIZE

BAND PATTERN ACTUAL SIZE

and cut it out. Place the pattern over the remaining dough and, using the knife, cut around it. Moisten the center of the rectangle by dipping your fingers into a little water and rubbing lightly. Place the heart in the center of the rectangle and press lightly with your fingers. Use the tines of a table fork to make impressions all around the heart—besides making an attractive edge, this will help to secure the heart to the rectangle.

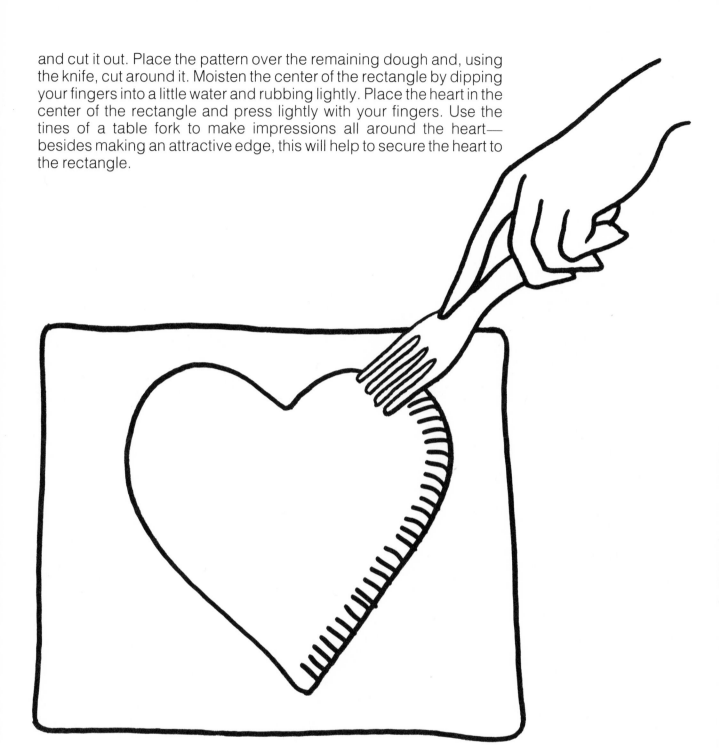

3. Trace the patterns for the bow and band shapes and cut them out. Place the patterns on the remaining dough and cut one bow and one band.

Also cut two strips that are ½ inch wide and 14 inches long, using the ruler to guide the knife blade as you cut. Lightly moisten one side of each strip; with that side against the rectangle, arrange the strips so that they intersect in the center of the heart, as shown. As you place the strips, loosely "ruffle" them to give a ribboned effect. Then cut a V

shape at the end of each ribbon. Wrap the bow's band section around
the bow shape, as shown, and lightly moisten the back of the bow.

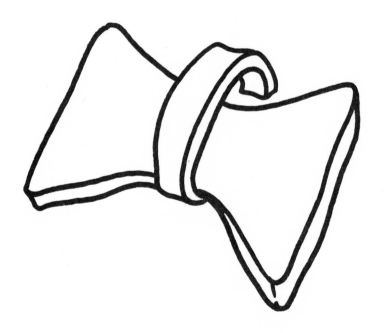

Place it in the center of the heart directly over the intersecting ribbons and press lightly.

4. To make a glaze, place the egg yolk in a cup and blend in 1 teaspoon of water. Using the watercolor brush, paint the glaze evenly over the heart. Add one drop of red food coloring to the remaining glaze and brush this over the remaining areas of the valentine. Give the bow an even pinker color by brushing it with a second coat of tinted glaze after the first has dried.

5.To prevent the valentine from puffing up during baking, use the knife to prick holes through the heart and the straight pin through all the other areas. Bake the valentine in a preheated 325-degree F. oven for 30 to 40 minutes, or until the edges are lightly browned and baker's clay is crisp. Remove it from the oven and let it cool on the cookie sheet.

6. Coat the back side of the valentine with white glue and attach the felt piece; allow the glue to dry completely before hanging it.

Mardi Gras

A great many of our festive days have originated in the Mediterranean area, many of which are part of Christian or pagan celebrations. Mardi Gras (literally, "Fat Tuesday")—the last big feast before the forty days of Lenten fasting and church-going—is one of these. Mardi Gras, or Carnival, in some countries has expanded its celebrations to last a full week or even a month before Lent, with parades and feasting and glittering costumes and decorations. In the United States, Mardi Gras centers in New Orleans; in the Caribbean Islands, it is in Trinidad that Carnival is explosive; and farther south, the Carnival capital is Rio de Janeiro. In France, the parade in Nice with its larger-than-life-size puppets is justly famous for its extravagance.

Regardless of where one celebrates Mardi Gras, there is always a sense of make-believe. If you're celebrating at home, hang our sparkling silver chandelier in the center of the ceiling for your Mardi Gras night. It will sway in any small breeze, catching and reflecting light in shimmering patterns. To complete the fantasy, serve the Crown Royale dessert—a molded, frozen confection fit for the crowned king and queen of the Mardi Gras.

SPARKLING CHANDELIER

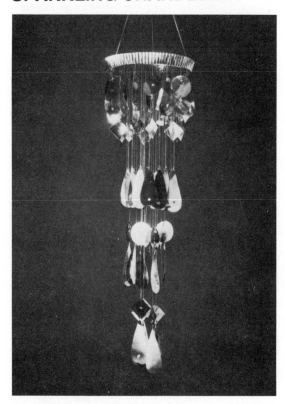

Tools and Materials

compass
1 sheet paper, 14 × 14 inches, in white
scissors
metal flan pan with fluted edges, 12 inches in diameter
1 piece plywood, 12 × 12 inches
nail
hammer
1 yard metallic cord, in silver
heavy needle
5 packages 6-strand embroidery thread, in gray
64 small buttons, each ½ to ⅝ inch in diameter
tracing paper, 8½ × 11 inches
white glue
lightweight cardboard
2 sheets 2-ply bristol board, each 20 × 30 inches
6 yards Contact paper, in silver
felt-tipped marking pen, in black
#1 X-acto knife with #11 blades
Duco or Welco household cement
4 packages glitter

Instructions

1. Using the compass, draw a circle 10 inches in diameter on the
paper. Then draw four more circles inside the 10-inch circle, making

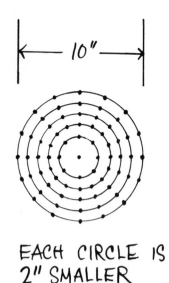

← 10" →

EACH CIRCLE IS
2" SMALLER

each one 2 inches smaller in diameter than the one before, as shown in the illustration. Add the dots equidistantly around each circumference, following the same illustration for the number of dots needed in each case. Cut out the circle on the 10-inch line and lay it on the bottom of the flan pan.

2. Place the flan pan on the piece of plywood. With nail and hammer, punch small holes through the bottom of the flan pan, following the paper pattern for placement.

3. Still using the hammer and nail, make three evenly spaced holes around the outside edge of the pan. Cut the silver cord into three equal pieces. Knot one end of each cord through one of the holes. Tie the free ends of the cords together so that the piece can be hung— the pan should be right side up. Hang the piece from a hook before proceeding with the next step.

4. Measure and cut the embroidery thread into the following lengths. Each piece is actually 3 inches longer than it needs to be to allow for tying the top end to a button and the bottom to a pendant.

    A. 16 pieces, 3¾ inches long
    B. 16 pieces, 10½ inches long
    C. 16 pieces, 15½ inches long
    D.   8 pieces, 22 inches long
    E.   8 pieces, 31¾ inches long

5. With a heavy needle, thread the A lengths through the outer circle of holes, bringing them up from the bottom of the pan to the top. Thread a button on each length and hold it in position by tying the end of the thread in a knot. The other end should hang free. Add the remaining pieces of embroidery thread in the same way until all threads have been attached, following the letters indicated on the pattern and ending up with the E pieces in the center.

6. Trace the patterns for the teardrop, circle, and diamond shapes on tracing paper, glue them to pieces of cardboard, and cut them out.

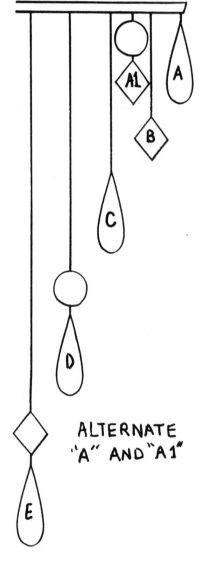

ALTERNATE
"A" AND "A1"

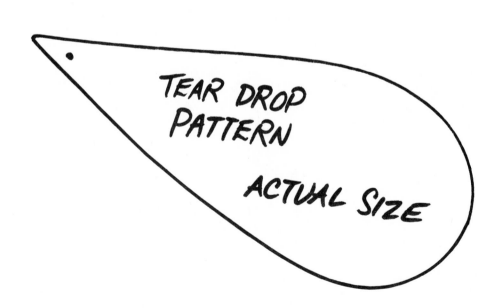

TEAR DROP
PATTERN
ACTUAL SIZE

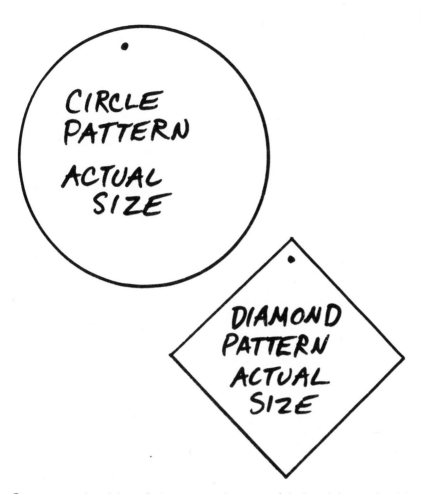

CIRCLE PATTERN ACTUAL SIZE

DIAMOND PATTERN ACTUAL SIZE

7. Cover each side of the two sheets of bristol board with silver Contact paper, following the manufacturer's directions. Lay the cardboard patterns on the covered board and trace around them with the marking pen, making thirty-eight teardrops, fifteen circles, and fifty-eight diamonds in all. Cut out the shapes with the X-acto knife, holding it as you would a pencil, drawing it toward yourself to cut, and pressing firmly enough to cut cleanly through the board with one stroke.

8. Place a drop of cement in the center of one side of each pendant and sprinkle it with glitter. Allow the glue to dry and then repeat the procedure on the other side.

9. Punch a small hole in the top of each pendant with a thin nail or the heavy needle. Some pendants should also have a hole at the bottom. See the pattern in step 5 for these shapes.

10. Working from the center out, attach the diamond-shaped pendants to the free ends of the longest threads, tying each shape in place securely and making sure that each thread is the correct length. Attach a teardrop shape to the bottom of each diamond with another short length of embroidery thread so that they are about ⅜ inch apart. Following the pattern, attach all the other shapes to the threads. Do not be concerned if the threads become tangled or twist around each other as you work—this is the nature of the project and it will resolve itself in the end.

ICE CREAM CROWN ROYALE

To make this dessert, you must begin the preparation the day before you wish to serve it (see steps 1 and 2 below). You also need a freezer that is both large and cold. It must be large enough to accommodate a 12-inch-round serving tray plus eight 8-inch-tall cones being held upright in small glasses. It must also be cold enough to freeze the ice cream to a solid mass. To serve this frozen masterpiece, cut it with a sharp serrated knife. Makes thirty-two 6-ounce servings.

Tools and Materials

3 cartons (½ gallon each) rippled ice cream (we used chocolate)
8 squares aluminum foil, each 8 × 8 inches
transparent tape
scissors
1 Bundt mold or angelfood cake pan, 10 inches in diameter
round serving tray, 12 inches in diameter
8 small glasses, such as heavy shot glasses or juice glasses
8 toothpicks
pastry bag with #30 star tip
1 cup heavy cream, whipped

Instructions

1. Begin preparations the day before you wish to serve this dessert.

Irish Coffee Mousse

Ice Cream Crown Royale

58

Cauliflower Lamb and Vegetable Flowers

Greek Flowerpot

Fake-Fur Bunny

Heart-Shaped Cherry Pie

60

Wooden Frog Planter

A Potpourri Heart

Stenciled Shamrock T-Shirt

A Raindrop Umbrella

A Photo Collage

63

Hand-Painted Easter Eggs

Thaw ice cream for 15 minutes while preparing aluminum foil cones. To make the cones, fold the eight squares of aluminum foil diagonally into eight triangles. Shape each into a cone, as shown, and secure with tape along the seams. Trim each with scissors as shown.

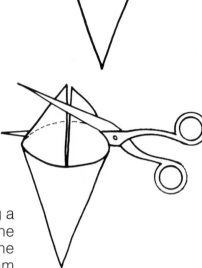

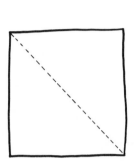 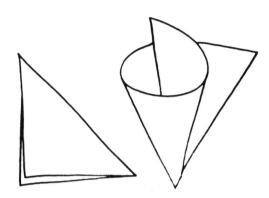

2. Fill the Bundt mold with ice cream and then fill the cones: Using a large spoon, scoop the ice cream from the carton and pack it into the mold. Place the scoops that have the nicest swirls or ripples along the wall of the mold so that they will be facing outward when the ice cream is unmolded. Continue packing the mold until the ice cream is flush with the top of the mold. Turn the freezer temperature control to its coldest position and place the mold in the freezer. Using a small spoon, pack the cones with ice cream, placing the swirls along the wall of each cone so that they will face outward when the cones are unmolded. Place the pointed end of each filled cone into a small galss and place in freezer. Freeze all ice cream shapes 12 hours or over-night before proceeding.

3. Fill a sink with 4 inches of hot tap water. Submerge the mold into the water so that it almost reaches the top, and hold it there for 5 seconds. Remove the mold from the water and quickly dry the out-side. Place the serving tray upside down over the mold and, holding both together, invert them. Lightly tap the mold; the ice cream should easily unmold onto the tray. Place in freezer for 2 hours or until any softened ice cream refreezes.

4. Remove ice cream shape on the tray from the freezer and place it on a work surface. The Bundt mold will have formed eight convex shapes around the shape; each of these will hold one ice cream cone. Push a toothpick partway into the ice cream in the center of each convex area. Working with one cone at a time—leave the rest in the freezer—invert it over one of the toothpicks so that the pointed end is up. Remove the tape holding the foil and peel away the foil. Working quickly, add the remaining cones in this way. If you used an angel-food cake pan for your mold, simply add the cones equally spaced around the diameter. Place the entire Crown Royale in the freezer for 3 to 4 hours or until all is frozen solid.

5. Fill the pastry bag with the whipped cream and, following the project photograph, pipe a scalloped border of rosettes around each cone, following the outer curves of the cones. Also pipe a shell border around the base of the crown. *Makes thirty-two 6-ounce servings.*

5

St. Patrick's Day

St. Patrick, the patron saint of Ireland, has given his name to this holiday that long ago crossed the ocean to the United States and is now celebrated on March 17th across the country with the "wearin' of the green" and the shamrock—which, legend has it, represents the Trinity. It was the Irish who brought their memories, the marching bands, and the Irish songs with them when they settled in New York and Boston and Philadelphia, eventually spreading across the continent.

Of course, you don't have to be Irish to enjoy wearing our shamrock-printed T-shirt, with its bright green design against white cotton, or eating our Irish Coffee Mousse, a fabulous dessert that will warm the cockles of your heart on any day.

STENCILED SHAMROCK T-SHIRT

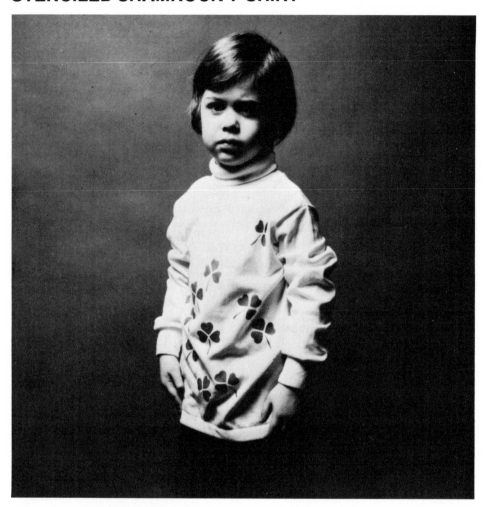

Tools and Materials

ruler
fine felt-tipped marking pen, in black
1 sheet tracing paper, 9 × 12 inches
white glue
2 sheets uncorrugated cardboard, each 9 × 12 inches
1 sheet stencil paper, 18 × 24 inches
scissors
masking tape
#1 X-acto knife with #11 blades
cotton T-shirt, in white
newspapers
1 tube acrylic paint, in permanent green light
paper plate (for a palette)
#5 stencil brush
paper towels

Instructions

1. Using the marking pen, trace the shamrock pattern on the tracing
paper.

67

ACTUAL
SIZE

2. Glue the tracing-paper design to one sheet of cardboard and allow the glue to dry thoroughly.

3. With scissors, cut several rectangles of stencil paper, each slightly larger than the stencil design.

4. Place one stencil-paper rectangle over the shamrock design and tape it in place.

5. Holding the X-acto knife exactly as you would a pencil, cut along the marking-pen lines showing through the semitransparent stencil paper. Always cut toward yourself, allowing the knife to "flow" over the lines of the design, and cut *just* through the stencil paper. Remove the stencil and set it aside. Repeat the procedure, cutting several shamrock stencils in all.

6. Plan the design for your T-shirt by making a rough sketch of it on a piece of scrap paper first. Plan it to the size of the area that you want to cover on the T-shirt. The child's T-shirt shown in the photograph is patterned with twelve shamrocks placed at random angles to each other with one shamrock on a sleeve.

7. Place a pile of folded newspapers on the working surface. Put the second sheet of cardboard inside the T-shirt so that the paint will not bleed through to the back of the shirt.

8. Referring to your rough sketch, position one of the stencils on the shirt to make the first shamrock.

9. Squeeze a small amount of green paint on the paper plate; then pick up a little of it on the end of the brush. Always make sure that the brush you are using is clean and dry. "Pounce" the brush up and down on several layers of newspapers to remove excess paint while evenly distributing the paint throughout the bristles.

10. Holding the stencil firmly in place with one hand, use the other to dab the brush in a gentle up-and-down motion through the openings in the stencil design. When all the openings of the design have been covered evenly with paint, quickly lift the stencil away from the fabric, picking it straight up so as not to smear the edges of the design. Wash out the brush in a bowl of water, wipe it clean with paper towels, let it dry, and repeat the procedure until the design is complete.

11. When the stencil gets soaked with paint and the edges lose their definition, substitute a new stencil so that the edges of the design will stay sharp and clean and there is no chance of the cloth's becoming smudged with excess paint.

IRISH COFFEE MOUSSE

Makes eight 5-ounce servings.

Tools and Materials

aluminum foil
8 tall, straight-sided, after-dinner coffee cups, 4-ounce size
butter
rubber bands
Irish Coffee Mousse (recipe follows)
chocolate sprinkles
fresh clover or shamrocks (optional)

Instructions

1. Prepare the coffee cups before beginning the mousse. For each, cup, you will need a strip of aluminum foil 2½ inches wide and long enough to wrap around the top of each cup. Lightly butter one side of each strip, and wrap each one around a cup, making sure that the buttered side is facing the inside of the cup. The foil should cover the outside of the top edge of each cup to a depth of 1 inch and extend 1½ inches above the rim of the cup. Hold each strip in place with a rubber band. Set the cups aside while you make the mousse.

IRISH COFFEE MOUSSE

1 envelope unflavored gelatin
⅓ cup sugar
2 tablespoons instant coffee
2 tablespoons cornstarch
2 eggs, separated
3 tablespoons Irish whisky
5 tablespoons sugar
1 cup heavy (whipping) cream

Combine 1¾ cups cold water, the gelatin, and the ⅓ cup sugar in a medium saucepan. Bring to a boil, stirring occasionally, and simmer 2 to 3 minutes. Remove from heat and stir in the instant coffee. Place the cornstarch in a small bowl and stir in ¼ cup cold water. Add cornstarch mixture to coffee mixture and simmer, stirring constantly, until thickened. Beat egg yolks lightly and slowly add them to the coffee mixture as you beat rapidly with a whisk or fork. Keep the heat low so that the mixture doesn't curdle. Cook until mixture thickens, about 1 minute. Remove from heat and stir in the Irish whisky. Pour mixture into a large mixing bowl and cool thoroughly but do not refrigerate or gelatin will set. Beat the egg whites in a medium mixing bowl. When almost stiff, gradually add 3 tablespoons sugar and continue beating until stiff. Fold the egg whites carefully into the coffee mixture. In another bowl, beat the cream until it is almost stiff. Gradually add the remaining 2 tablespoons of sugar, beating until thick. Carefully fold the whipped cream into the cooled mousse mixture. Divide the mousse among the prepared cups, filling each up to the top of the aluminum foil collar. Chill overnight or until set. To serve, run a sharp knife around the inside of each aluminum foil collar and then carefully remove it. Using your fingers, press some chocolate sprinkles around the top outside edge of each mousse. Just before serving, place a fresh clover or shamrock on top of each mousse if you wish. *Makes 8 servings.*

Easter

The Easter legend is very close to the Christian religion, yet many parts of it are even older—the ancient pagan rites of spring and the growing season, of sowing seed, of planting crops, and of newborn animals rising on wobbly legs in the fields. The pagan goddess Ester is linked to all these customs ritualized by the eastern Mediterranean, all of which are part of our heritage—no matter what our national backgrounds, some of these customs are now incorporated into our own family traditions.

Our fake-fur rabbit is our version of the Easter bunny who leaves baskets of colored, dappled, and flecked eggs for the children to find. Flowering plants—whether tulips or lilies—are natural symbols of rebirth; our flowerpot, with its bold Greek design, will show them off to best advantage. The symbol of the lamb appears in many legends, often represented by a molded sweet cake iced with white sugar frosting. Our lamb, made of cauliflower and eggplant and surrounded by vegetable flowers, is a centerpiece for the Easter feast. With an accompanying dip for vegetables, the lamb will also serve as an appetizing way to begin the festivities.

CAULIFLOWER LAMB AND VEGETABLE FLOWERS

If you wish, you can make the vegetable flowers for this project the night before and keep them in the refrigerator in a bowl of ice water until serving time. When that time arrives, make a bowl or two of your favorite vegetable dips to accompany the cauliflower lamb and vegetable flowers.

Tools and Materials

long, sharp knife
1 block of Styrofoam, approximately 6 × 6 × 11 inches (if this size is not available, glue several chunks together)
plastic wrap
ruler
1 eggplant, approximately 1 pound
toothpicks
4 medium-size heads of cauliflower
large platter
11 radishes: 5 small, 3 medium-size, and 3 large
vegetable peeler
3 carrots: 2 large and 1 small
1 medium-size white turnip

Instructions

1. Using the sharp knife, shape the Styrofoam block so that it looks

like the illustrations. The beveled end of the block will become the tail end of the lamb.

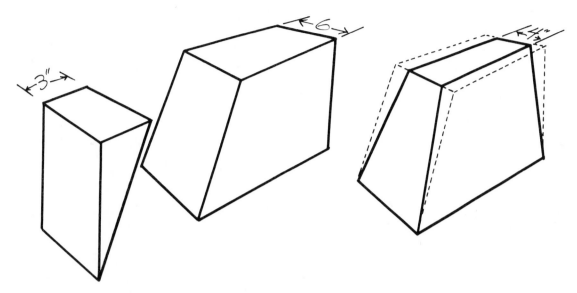

2. Cover the Styrofoam shape with clear plastic wrap so that no food will come in contact with it.

3. To make the nose, cut away the wide end of the eggplant so that 3½ to 4 inches of the stem end remains. (Save the wide end to make the

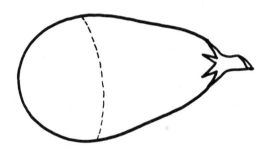

ears and tail.) Insert four toothpicks partway into the cut part of the eggplant nose and thrust the other ends into the top half of the Styrofoam square opposite the tail section.

4. Wash the cauliflower and separate it into florets. Place a toothpick partway into each cauliflower floret and insert the other end into the Styrofoam, covering the entire block and using the largest pieces of cauliflower around the nose and tail sections,

5. Make the ears as follows: Cut the blunt portion of the eggplant in half, as shown in the illustration, and then cut out two ear shapes. Carve away most of the pulp so that the ears are thin and mostly peel. Secure one ear on each side of the nose with toothpicks.

6. Cut a few strips of the remaining eggplant to make a tail, and, with toothpicks, attach the strips to the back of the lamb.

7. Cut a small radish into two thin crosswise slices to make the eyes. Use half a toothpick to secure each to the eggplant face.

8. Use another toothpick to attach a whole, small radish for the nose.

9. To make the mouth, cut a thin, lengthwise slice from the thickest part of a carrot. Using a small sharp knife, cut it into the shape shown

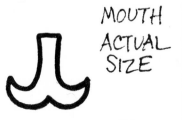

MOUTH
ACTUAL
SIZE

73

in the illustration. Push mouth onto half a toothpick and insert the toothpick into the eggplant below the nose.

10. Place the lamb on a large platter and set aside while you make the vegetable flowers.

Carrot Chrysanthemums:

11. Remove the skin of the large carrots with a vegetable peeler, and cut away both ends, leaving a 5-inch length of the thickest part of the carrots.

12. With a very sharp knife, cut into the carrots lengthwise to make as many thin slices as possible. (It is best to practice this on a couple of extra carrots first.) For each chrysanthemum, you will need three thin slices.

13. Starting in the center of each slice and working toward each end, make four lengthwise cuts through each carrot slice, ending each cut

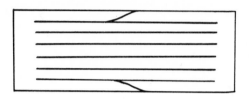

¾ inch from each edge. Then make two angled cuts at each side, as shown.

14. Bend each slice as shown in the illustration and secure with a toothpick, as shown in the illustration.

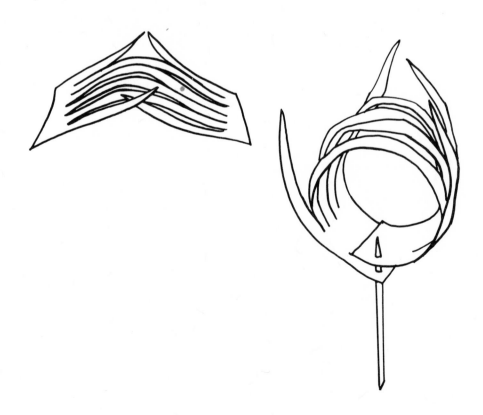

15. For each flower, attach three bent carrot slices to one toothpick, using a small crosswise carrot slice to hold the last one in place, as shown.

16. Place the chrysanthemums in ice water for at least an hour to help them "fluff up."

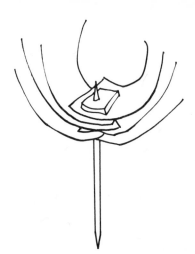

Radish Roses:

17. Trim away the stem end and tip of each radish. For each radish rose, you will need one large, one medium, and one small radish.

18. Slice the medium and small radishes into crosswise slices no thicker than ⅛ inch.

19. Insert a toothpick ½ inch into the stem end of each large radish.

20. Beginning near the stem end of each large radish and working toward the root tip, bring the knife down vertically to make ½-inch-wide curving cuts, ¼ inch deep all round, turning the radish as you work and staggering the cuts. When you get to the root tip, make three straight cuts down into the flat surface where the root has been cut away, forming a center triangle, as shown.

21. To make the petals, insert the radish slices into the cuts. Use the largest slices for the bottom of the rose and work upward, using progressively smaller slices. Reserve the three smallest slices for the cuts on the top.

22. Place radish roses in ice water for at least one hour before serving.

Turnip Daisies:

23. Cut a practice daisy before you begin: Peel the turnip with a vegetable peeler, and slice it crosswise into ¼-inch-thick slices. Each slice will become a daisy.

24. Following the illustrations, make six or seven petals from each slice by cutting away areas of it, leaving a circle of uncut turnip approximately ¾ inch in diameter in the center.

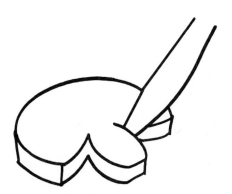

Turn the turnip slightly each time you cut and cut each petal to exactly the same shape. Leave the tip of each petal uncut so that it has a flat edge.

25. As each daisy is completed, insert half a toothpick through the center and push a small carrot slice on the end to make the daisy center.

26. Place the daisies in ice water for at least an hour.

FAKE FUR BUNNY

Tools and Materials

pencil
ruler
tracing paper, 8½ × 11 inches
scissors
½ yard fake rabbit fur, in gray
1 piece velveteen, 10 × 10 inches, in pink (for ears and nose)
straight pins
nylon quilt-stuffing material
thread, in gray
carpet thread, in gray (optional)
2 needles: one regular and one carpet (optional)
sewing machine
2 buttons, each ⅜ to ½ inch in diameter, in black (for eyes)
lightweight wire (for stiffening ears)
masking tape
1 piece fake fur, 3 × 3 inches, in white (for tail)
raffia or pipe cleaners, in tan

Instructions

1. Using the ruler and pencil on the tracing paper, enlarge the pattern pieces by the grid method.

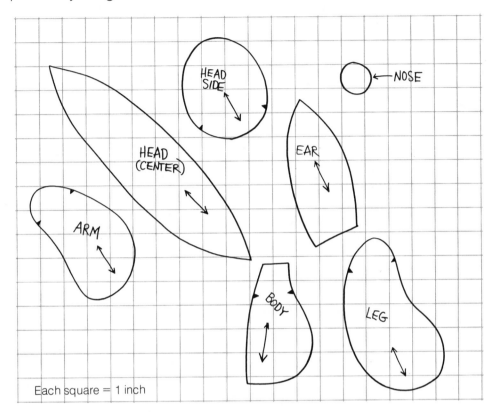

Each square = 1 inch

2. Pin pattern pieces to the wrong side of the fur and velveteen, making sure that the arrows follow the natural direction of the fur pile on the pieces to be cut out of the fur. When cutting the fake fur, cut it at an angle so that the fur strands won't get caught in the seams when the pieces are joined, although you will still have to pull some fur out from the seam with a needle or strong pin. Allowance has been made on the patterns for a ⅛-inch seam allowance all around. Cut the following number of fabric pieces from each pattern piece:

Head: One piece from fake fur

Sides of head: One piece from fake fur, turn pattern over, and cut one more piece

Ears: One piece from pink velveteen, turn pattern over, and cut one more piece. One piece from fake fur, turn pattern over, and cut one more piece

Body: Two pieces from fake fur, turn pattern over, and cut two more pieces

Arms: Two pieces from fake fur, turn pattern over, and cut two more pieces

Legs: Two pieces from fake fur, turn pattern over, and cut two more pieces

Nose: One piece from pink velveteen

3. Stitch the two head side pieces to the long head center, right sides

together. Leave an opening at the bottom. Turn inside out, stuff tightly, and sew up the open seam.

4. Tuck a small piece of stuffing material inside the wrong side of the velveteen for the nose. Sew small running stitches around the edge of the material and gather it by pulling the thread, making a round nose. Sew it to the face, turning the raw edges under the nose.

5. Sew on the buttons for eyes.

6. To make each ear, sew together one velveteen ear piece and one fur ear piece, with the right sides together. Leave the straight seam at the bottom open. Turn the ear right side out. Bend a small piece of wire into a long, looped shape and wrap the ends with masking tape so that they won't push through the fabric; place inside the ear. Tuck in the open edge on each ear and blind-stitch it to the head.

7. To make the body front, stitch the two fur pieces together along the straight edge, right sides together. Repeat for the body back. Stitch front to back, right sides together, leaving the top of the neck area open. Turn right side out, and stuff fully but not as tight and hard as the head—the body should be floppy and cuddly. Blind-stitch together the opening at the neck.

8. Make the arms and legs by stitching each two matching pieces together, right sides of fur facing each other; leave the small ends open. Turn the arms and legs right side out and stuff them loosely but fully. Tuck in all open edges, and blind-stitch together the openings on arms and legs.

9. Use double thread or carpet thread to stitch the body and head together so that the head is secure. Sew arms and legs to body so that they are floppy but still secure. Pull fur free of stitching so that the seams are covered.

10. Cut a 3-inch circle out of the white fake fur. Put stuffing in the center of the wrong side of the circle, sew around the edge, and then pull the loose thread to form a ball. Tuck the edges under and sew it to the body where the tail should be.

11. Use raffia or pipe cleaners for the whiskers. If you are using raffia, thread a length of it through a large-eyed needle and push it through from one side of the nose to the other. Pull enough raffia through so that the whisker is the same length on each side of the nose. Add as many whiskers as you wish in this way. If you are using pipe cleaners, make small holes in the face with scissors and push each pipe cleaner through from one side to the other.

GREEK FLOWERPOT

Tools and Materials

paintbrush, 2 inches wide
unglazed clay flowerpot, 11 inches in top diameter
marine varnish or polyurethane
pencil
ruler
tracing paper, 8½ × 11 inches
1 sheet carbon paper, 8½ × 11½ inches
masking tape
felt-tipped waterproof marking pen, in black
1 tube (2 ounces) acrylic paint, in black
2 paper plates
2 watercolor brushes: one #4 and one #12
1 piece cardboard, 5 × 5 inches, in white
1 piece stencil paper, 4 × 4 inches
#1 X-acto knife with #11 blades
stencil brush, #4

Instructions

1. Using the 2-inch brush, coat the inside of the pot with two coats of

marine varnish or polyurethane, allowing the first coat to dry thoroughly before proceeding with the next.

2. Trace the figure on a piece of tracing paper and tape it to the nontransferring side of the carbon paper.

ACTUAL SIZE

3. Tape the design and the carbon paper to the flowerpot. Make sure that the transferring side of the carbon is against the pot. With the pencil, trace over the design, transferring it to the surface of the pot. Before you remove the design, untape one side and carefully lift up the edge to make sure that you have transferred the entire image. Repeat this step four more times equidistantly around the pot.

4. Lay the pot on its side and, with the black marking pen, go over all the carbon lines.

5. Mask out the underside of the pot rim and then run your fingernail over the tape to make sure that it is firmly adhered.

6. Squeeze a small amount of black paint on a paper plate and mix it with enough water to give it the consistency of thick cream. Using the #4 watercolor brush, outline each figure with at least a ¼-inch-wide band of black paint. Then use the #12 watercolor brush to fill in the rest of the background with black paint, painting up onto the masking tape. Let dry and then pull off the masking tape.

7. Trace the floral design with the black marker, and glue it to the piece of cardboard.

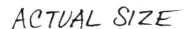

8. Tape the stencil paper over the design. Using the X-acto knife, cut out the design components showing through the stencil paper. Holding the knife as you would a pencil, draw it toward you, flowing over the surface as the knife point cuts through the stencil paper.

9. Brace the pot on its side. Tape the stencil onto the lip of the flowerpot, making sure that the lower edge of the design is ¼ inch above the lower edge of the rim.

10. Squeeze a small amount of black paint on the second paper plate but do not dilute it with water. Dip the tip of the stencil brush into the paint and then pounce the brush on some newspaper to remove excess paint. Remember that the brush should be fairly dry—too much paint will run under the edge of the stencil, creating a messy design.

11. Begin to stencil the design by dabbing the paint through the stencil openings with an up-and-down dabbing motion. When all the openings have been filled with paint, carefully lift up the stencil. Let the design dry for a moment or two, until dry to the touch.

12. Reposition the stencil to the right of the design just stenciled, placing it so that the right-hand side of the black design appears through the opening on the left-hand side of the stencil. Remember to keep the design ¼ inch up from the lower edge of the rim.

13. Stencil as before, and then repeat this step until the entire rim has been stenciled. Let dry.

14. Fill the pot with soil and a plant.

HAND-PAINTED EASTER EGGS

Tools and Materials

eggs, some with brown shells and some with white
paper towels
facial tissues
nontoxic watercolors, in red, yellow, blue, green, brown, rust, and
    green
2 watercolor brushes: one #3 and one #8
vegetable oil

Instructions

1. Allow the eggs to sit at room temperature for 1 hour and then hard-cook them: Place them in a large pan or Dutch oven and cover them with cold water. Then bring the water to a simmer, uncovered, over medium heat. Turn the heat to high and bring the water to a boil; turn off the heat and allow the eggs to remain in the water for 25 minutes. Rinse them in cold water. If any have cracked, reserve them for another use.

2. Cover a work surface with paper towels. Fill a bowl with water and assemble all remaining materials. Then, following the instructions in the following steps, begin to color the backgrounds of the eggs.

3. Place each white egg on a facial tissue and paint it entirely with one

medium color of watercolor, using the #8 watercolor brush. Paint some of the backgrounds medium blue, some pink, some yellow, and the rest light green. Holding the ends of the tissue as shown in the illustration, slightly lift the egg and gently let it roll back and forth; this will help to blot away some of the color and make an interesting texture. You may do the same with a paper towel if you wish the

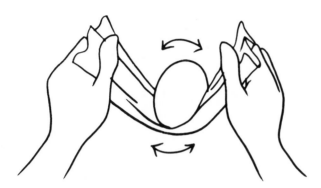

texture of the paper towel to show on an egg. Then let each egg dry completely on its tissue.

4. Using the #8 brush for large spots and the #3 brush for smaller spots, use a dabbing motion to make a speckled effect on some areas of each egg; leave other areas plain. Create a spattered effect on some of the eggs by dipping the #8 brush into some watercolor and then hitting the handle of the brush against your finger. Eggs with a blue background look best with darker blue spots and a few brown spots; pink eggs look best with red spots and a few brown spots, although a few green or blue spots will also enhance pink backgrounds; yellow eggs look best with brown spots.

5. Place each brown egg on a tissue and paint the backgrounds rust or dark brown. Then roll each around on its tissue, as described in step 3, to blot the color. Following the method described in step 4, paint darker brown and some dark blue spots on the eggs; create a spattered effect with darker brown and blues.

6. When all the eggs—both brown and white—are dry, add white and light brown spots to some of them. To do this, dip a clean #8 brush in clean water. Paint a spot and then blot it with a clean tissue. This blotting procedure will remove all the color, leaving a white spot on white eggs and a light brown spot on brown eggs. Remember that most eggs will look best if some areas have spots and others don't.

7. To "set" the color and give each egg a sheen, apply vegetable oil to a paper towel and then wipe the surface of the egg. Because oil and water don't mix, the oil will not affect the designs you have made. Let the oiled eggs dry for an hour and then wipe them again with a clean paper towel.

7

May Day

May Day, and, of course, the month of May itself, derives its name from the goddess Maia. Related to ancient Roman customs, May Day is one of the numerous rites of spring. And there is nothing more springlike than the first warm days of the year with the faint smell of green leaves, grass, and warm earth.

The occasion calls for a party that recognizes May—and spring in general—for what it is, a fickle season of green things growing and surprise rain showers. The wooden frog planter with its splashy green and tan spots is a perfect holder for a lushly growing fern, a portent of summer days to come. And for protection from those random cloudbursts, try our skyblue umbrella covered with white raindrops.

WOODEN FROG PLANTER

Tools and Materials

3 sheets tracing or typewriter paper, each 8½ × 11 inches
masking tape
3 sheets carbon paper, each 8½ × 11½ inches
ruler
hard pencil
jigsaw
1 piece pine, ¾ inch thick × 12 inches wide × approximately 7 feet
  long
white glue
finishing nails
hammer
medium sandpaper
5 tubes acrylic paints: one each in permanent green light, yellow
  ochre, cadmium yellow medium, white, and black
2 paintbrushes: one 1 inch wide and one fine-pointed
old toothbrush

Instructions

1. Tape the three sheets of tracing paper together side by side along
their long edges; repeat with the three sheets of carbon paper. Using

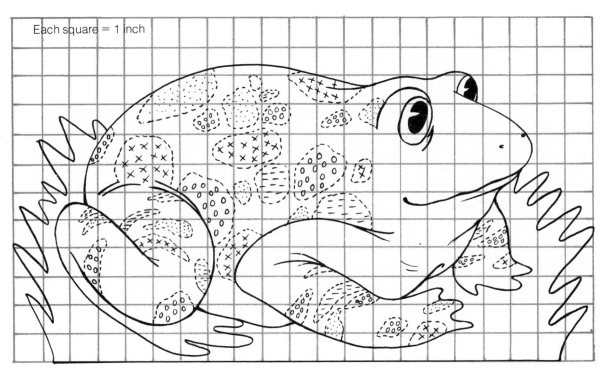

Each square = 1 inch

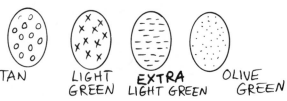

TAN   LIGHT GREEN   **EXTRA** LIGHT GREEN   OLIVE GREEN

the ruler and pencil on the tracing paper, enlarge the frog pattern by the grid method.

2. Using the jigsaw, cut two 22-inch lengths from the pine board.

3. Lay the carbon paper, carbon side down, on the better side of one 22-inch length of pine; lay the paper pattern on top. Trace around the outline and the design lines with the pencil, transferring the pattern to the wood. Flip the pattern over and trace a second frog on the other 22-inch length of pine. Both frogs should now face the same direction when cut out.

4. Cut out the two frog pieces with the jigsaw.

5. With the jigsaw, cut three more pieces from the remaining length of pine board: one 12 by 12 inches (for the bottom) and two 7 by 12 inches (for the front and back).

6. To assemble planter, center the 12- by 12-inch bottom piece between the two frog pieces. Make sure the frogs are facing the same direction. Glue and nail into place. Next, glue and nail, at a slant, the 7- by 12-inch front and back side pieces, following the diagram for proper placement. Let glue dry.

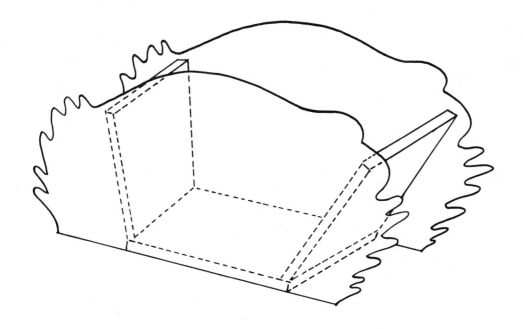

7. Lightly sand all surfaces.

8. Thin the permanent green light paint with enough water to make it the consistency of heavy cream. Then, using the 1-inch-wide brush, apply it to all surfaces of the three wooden pieces except where the frogs' spots should be and the grass.

9. Mix the colors for the spots:

    Light tan: 2 parts white with 1 part yellow ochre
    Light green: 1 part permanent green light with 1 part white
    Extra-light green: 1 part permanent green light with 2 parts white
    Olive green: 4 parts permanent green light with 1 part white and 1
      part black

10. Paint the spots on the frogs, following the color notes on the pattern. Let dry.

11. Mix each of the four colors for the spots with 2 parts of water to thin them out. Using the toothbrush and your finger, a fingernail, or a knife, splatter the colors all over each frog.

12. Paint the white part of the frogs' eyes with the fine brush. When dry, add the black pupil and eye outline. Then add the remainder of the outlines defining the frogs' bodies and legs, mouths, and nostrils.

13. Mix the color for the green grass: 2 parts cadmium yellow medium with 2 parts permanent green light, 2 parts white, and enough water to make it the consistency of heavy cream. Using free, curving strokes, paint the grass around the bottom of each frog.

A RAINDROP UMBRELLA

RAINDROP
PATTERN
ACTUAL SIZE

Tools and Materials

ruler
pencil
1 sheet tracing paper, 8½ × 11 inches
1 sheet carbon paper, 8½ × 11½ inches
file card, 3 × 5 inches, in white
scissors
masking tape, 1½ inches wide
1 yard Contact paper, in any color
felt-tipped or ballpoint pen
white umbrella with a ruffled edge
rubber cement (optional)
newspapers
2 spray cans (1 pint each) Krylon waterproof paint: one can in blue and
    one in deep blue

Instructions

1. With pencil on the tracing paper, trace the raindrop pattern. Transfer the design with carbon paper to the file card.
2. Cut out the raindrop design with scissors, starting at the pointed end. Once cut out, tape over the opening in the edge of the file card, as shown.

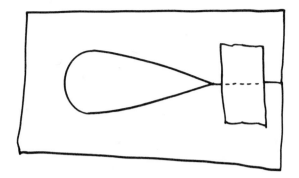

3. Lay the Contact paper on a work surface so that it is paper side up. Place the file card on top and trace around the outline of the raindrop with a felt-tipped or ballpoint pen.

4. Repeat the design, spacing the shapes about 1 inch apart to allow space for cutting out each raindrop with scissors. Make and cut out approximately seven dozen raindrops.

5. Mask out all areas on the umbrella not to be spray-painted—the ruffle, handle, and point.

6. One by one, peel off the paper backing from the raindrops and press them down on the open umbrella so that the broad part is toward the lower edge of the umbrella. Start at the top center point and work down, creating a loose pattern of raindrops over the entire umbrella. If the raindrops adhere poorly to the umbrella fabric, dab rubber cement on the sticky side to help hold the plastic to the material.

7. Spread sheets of newspaper over a work area in a well-ventilated place.

8. With the lighter blue spray paint, cover the umbrella, beginning at the lower edge. Turn the umbrella around as the spraying proceeds. For best results, spray lightly and quickly, holding the spray can no closer to the umbrella than a foot away. If more color is needed, spray over lightly again. Paint the umbrella's lower edge with a heavier application of color than the rest of the umbrella, keeping in mind to spray the top center area with only the lightest mist of blue paint.

9. When the surface has been covered and is dry to the touch, spray the lower edge of the umbrella with the darker blue paint. Again rotate the umbrella as the work proceeds, blending the edge of the paint so that there is no harsh line between the lighter and darker blue. It is always best to spray too lightly at first and, if more color is needed, spray over lightly again.

10. After the paint is dry, remove the self-adhesive plastic raindrops from the umbrella; also remove the masking tape from the ruffle, handle, and point.

8

Midsummer Night

In the northern countries where the sun shines almost all night on the 21st of June, Midsummer Night is a special holiday. It is the beginning of summer and the longest day of the year in the northern hemisphere. In Sweden and Norway, great bonfires are lighted at "night" to honor the sun, and celebrants gather to dance around the fire and drink toasts to the sun. Traditionally, strange events occur on Midsummer Night—the mischievous fairies are out, and the unsuspecting often find themselves the victims of playful tricks.

For a Midsummer Night's party, decorate a room with our "stained-glass" butterflies hung against the wall or suspended on thin threads from the ceiling so that the light will shine through their transparent wings. To honor the sun, concoct our sunburst-decorated punch, and welcome summer with a midnight celebration.

BIG BUTTERFLIES

Each of these butterflies is made by cutting two identical shapes from one sheet of black posterboard. The inside design is then cut away and filled by "sandwiching" colored cellophane between the two pieces.

Tools and Materials

tracing or thin typewriter paper, each 8½ × 11 inches
transparent tape
ruler
medium-hard pencil
white crayon pencil
3 sheets posterboard, each 22 × 28 inches, in black on both sides
#1 X-acto knife with #11 blades
fine sandpaper
cotton swabs
india ink, in black
fine watercolor brush
newspapers
transparent cellophane, in purple, red, yellow, green, orange, and
    blue, available by the foot or in rolls 20 × 60 inches or 20 × 150
    inches
scissors
acrylic gloss medium, such as Liquitex
6 pipe cleaners, each 11½ inches, in black

Instructions

1. Tape enough sheets of tracing or typing paper together to make two pieces that are large enough to accommodate the two enlarged butterfly patterns. Using the ruler and pencil on the sheets of paper,

18″

12″

Each square = 1 inch

Each square = 1 inch

enlarge each butterfly pattern by the grid method.

2. To transfer the patterns to the posterboard, first trace over all the lines of both patterns with the white crayon pencil, working *on the opposite side of the paper.* Lay the crayoned side against the black posterboard, and draw over the pattern lines with the pencil. Remove the pattern and go over any lines that are faint with the white pencil. To make the two smaller butterflies, draw the pattern four times on two sheets of posterboard. For the larger butterfly, draw the pattern twice on one sheet of posterboard.

3. Cut out all the shapes with the X-acto knife, holding it as you would a pencil, drawing it toward yourself to cut, and pressing firmly enough to cut cleanly through the posterboard with one stroke. Then cut away all shapes from the inside area of the wings. Cut carefully, for the wing outlines will become delicate as the board is cut away. Change X-acto blades frequently to ensure sharp, clean cuts and to avoid any chance of tearing the board.

4. When you have cut all six butterflies, smooth the rough edges with fine sandpaper. Color all cut edges with the cotton swabs dipped into black india ink. To color the sharp corners into which cotton swabs will not fit, use a fine brush with the ink.

5. Spread newspapers over a flat working surface or the floor. Lay one butterfly flat on the paper, with the better side facing down. Following the color notations on the diagrams, cut the cellophane to fit the inner

RED   ORANGE
PURPLE   BLUE
GREEN   YELLOW

wing shapes, allowing ¼ inch extra all around each shape.

6. Run a thin line of acrylic gloss medium around the edge of one of the cutout openings. Press the proper cellophane shape in place, smoothing the edges and removing any excess medium. Be very careful that none of the medium gets on the face of the cellophane. Continue applying cellophane in this way until all three butterfly shapes have been completed.

7. When all the cellophane has been glued into place, glue two pipe cleaners into place on the head of each butterfly to make antennae.

8. With the acrylic gloss medium, glue the remaining three black posterboard butterfly shapes, better sides up, into place over the three cellophane-covered butterflies, sandwiching the cellophane between two butterflies to make one. The result will be three butterflies with cellophane wings that resemble stained glass.

9. Lightly score the back of each butterfly using the ruler and the X-acto knife, following the line between the body and the wings; bend the wings slightly forward.

SUNBURST PUNCH

All the ingredients for this festive punch must be well chilled before the punch is prepared; the citrus sunburst decoration should be chilled for at least an hour before serving time. Makes forty-five 5-ounce servings.

Tools and Materials

Sunburst Punch (recipe follows)
3 medium-sized oranges
sharp knife
nontoxic wax crayon (optional)
1 medium-size grapefruit
toothpicks
maraschino cherry
tea towel or paper towels
aluminum foil
punch bowl
ice cubes

Instructions

1. Place all ingredients for the punch recipe (see step 6) into the

refrigerator until well chilled. Make the orange- and grapefruit-peel sunburst (see steps 2 through 5) at least one hour before the party and chill in the refrigerator.

2. Cut each of the three oranges into twelve pointed sections, as shown in the illustration. As you cut, use the sharp point of a kitchen

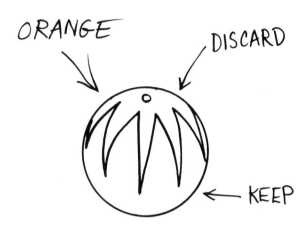

knife to cut through the peel but not into the orange. End each cut 1 inch from the bottom of the orange. If you are unsure of where to cut, lightly draw guidelines with a nontoxic wax crayon before cutting. After all cuts have been made, remove the top portion and discard. Using your fingers, pull out all the orange sections from within the peel and reserve for another use. Scrape the inside of the peel lightly with a small spoon if necessary.

3. Cut the grapefruit in half crosswise. Cut through the peel, barely into the grapefruit, to make six wedges of grapefruit peel, as shown.

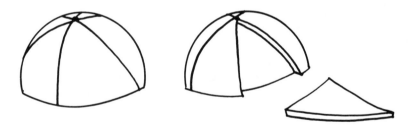

Remove them from the grapefruit sections and reserve the sections for another use.

4. Following the diagram, assemble the sunburst. Push on one orange peel, skin side up, so that it becomes slightly concave. With points up, rest the second orange peel on top of the concave portion. Secure the two peels together with three toothpicks inserted from the bottom. Invert the third peel on top of the second and arrange the twelve points so that each is between two below it.

5. Attach the twelve pointed sections of grapefruit peel between the points of the bottom orange, holding them in place by piercing each

with a toothpick inserted from the underside of the grapefruit peel into the orange peel. Attach one cherry to the top inverted orange, using half a toothpick. Moisten a clean tea towel or several paper towels

and lay them over a dinner plate. Place the sunburst on the towel, cover it loosely with aluminum foil, and refrigerate until you are ready to make the punch.

6. Make the punch:

SUNBURST PUNCH

1 quart orange juice (fresh if possible)
1 cup peach brandy
2 bottles (4/5 quart each) Sauterne wine
1 quart dry ginger ale
4 bottles (4/5 quart each) champagne
1 jar (10 ounces) maraschino cherries with liquid

Place the orange juice, brandy, and wine in the punch bowl and stir briefly. With the neck of the bottle resting on the rim of the punch bowl, slowly pour in the ginger ale and champagne. Stir punch once with a large spoon. Add some ice cubes and float the orange- and grapefruit-peel sunburst on top. Pour ½ cup maraschino cherry juice over the sunburst; do not stir. Garnish with additional maraschino cherries if desired. *Makes forty-five 5-ounce servings.*

Tiger Lilies and Gardenias

Oven-Baked Clay Jewelry

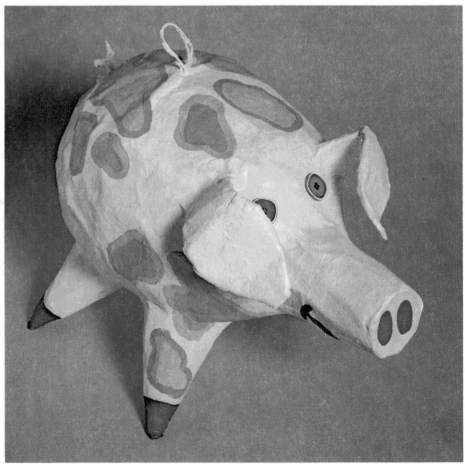

A Pinata Pig

98

tterflies

Frozen Pineapple Sticks

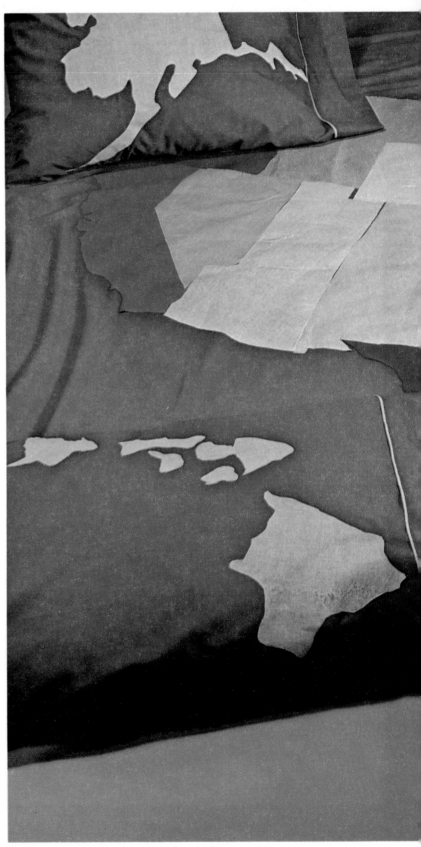

Map Picnic Cloth

Batik American Flag

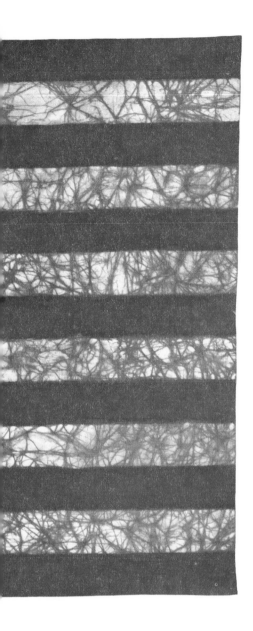

Alphabet Soup Message Gift Box and Card

Sunburst Punch

9

Patriotic Holidays

Throughout the year there are patriotic holidays—Washington's Birthday, Lincoln's Birthday, Memorial Day, Fourth of July, Labor Day, Veterans' Day—each with its own set of legends and special celebrations, featuring cherry pies and hatchets, stovepipe hats, fireworks and marching bands, memorial wreaths of flowers—but throughout our national celebrations run two themes—our country and our flag.

To celebrate all patriotic holidays, we have made a picnic-cloth map of the United States—all fifty states with Hawaii and Alaska on the pillowcases. Either stuff the pillows for sitting on or use them for carrying picnic goodies to an outing. And you can be sure that the children (and adults) will spend some of their picnic time identifying states, remembering friends in different parts of the country, following the route of car, railroad, bus, and plane trips they've taken. The batik flag is just right to hang from a flagpole in the front yard or drape from a window or the front porch railing, or to wave happily over a back yard barbecue.

MAP PICNIC CLOTH

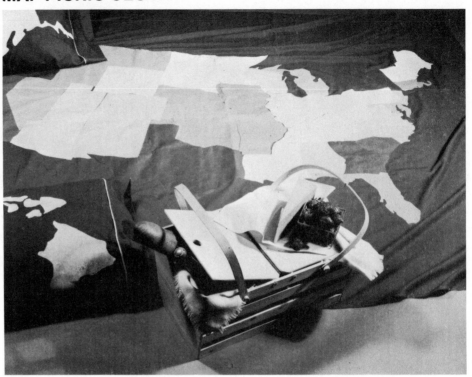

Tools and Materials

ruler
pencil
classic Hammond map of the United States, approximately 2 × 4 feet
    (available in variety and stationery stores)
1 sheet brown wrapping paper, 4 × 8 feet
2 sheets brown wrapping paper, each 20 × 27 inches
scissors
1 flat, double-size, no-iron bed sheet, in dark blue
chalk
10 yards Stitch-witchery
10 yards polyester/cotton fabric: 1 yard each in beige, light blue, light
    brown, light green, medium green, pink, red, rust, yellow, and yellow
    mustard
straight pins
iron
permanent felt-tipped marking pen (optional)
2 no-iron pillowcases, in dark blue

Instructions

1. Using the ruler and pencil, mark the map off in 3-inch squares so
that you will be able to enlarge it to the size of the bed sheet by the grid
method. Measure off 6-inch squares on the 4- by 8-foot sheet of
paper. Working square by square, copy the outline of the United
States from the map to the paper and then outline the states except
Hawaii and Alaska. In the same way, enlarge Hawaii on one of the 20-

by 27-inch sheets of paper; enlarge Alaska on the other. Each of these two states will be applied to one of the pillowcases. Cut out all three patterns on their outlines.

2. Plan the color scheme for the overall map, using contrasting colors for each state or for groups of states. Since the background is dark blue, you may want to use the lighter colors along the coastlines. Mark the paper pattern with the colors chosen for each area.

3. Lay the bed sheet out flat and center the map pattern on top. Carefully draw around the outline with a piece of chalk; set sheet aside.

4. Make pattern pieces by cutting up the large paper pattern of the United States into the separate states or groups of states according to color.

5. Cut the Stitch-witchery into ten 1-yard pieces. Lay one of the pieces on top of one of the pieces of fabric. Pin a pattern piece designated to be of that color fabric on top and cut around it, cutting through both layers. Repeat this procedure until all the shapes have been cut of the appropriate colors.

6. Lay the sheet flat on the floor. Position the states or groups of states with the layer of Stitch-witchery underneath within the chalk outline you drew on the sheet and carefully pin them in place, using as many pins as you need to prevent the fabric and Stitch-witchery from shifting.

7. Following the manufacturer's directions for using Stitch-witchery, iron on all the separate pieces. If you have grouped several states together, outline the separate states with a marking pen if desired.

8. Pin the fabric pieces, with the Stitch-witchery underneath, for Hawaii and Alaska to the pillowcases, centering one state on each. Again following manufacturer's directions, bond the two fabrics together. Stuff the finished pillowcases with pillow stuffing and sew them together along the open edge, insert pillows into them, or use them to tote picnic gear.

BATIK AMERICAN FLAG

Our flag is made in two pieces, which are dyed separately and then sewn together. The finished flag measures 29¼ by 46½ inches.

Tools and Materials

yardstick
pencil
1 flat, twin-size, no-iron bed sheet, in white
scissors
1 sheet tracing paper, 8½ × 11 inches
1 sheet uncorrugated cardboard, 8½ × 11 inches
white glue
1 pound beeswax
paraffin (household wax used for canning)
large metal can, such as a coffee can
metal pan large enough to hold can plus water
baking soda
small artist's paintbrush (for applying wax)
newspapers or pad of newsprint
cold water dyes: 2 ounces each in blue and red
2 basins (for the dye baths)
iron
straight pins
needle or sewing machine
clear nylon thread

Instructions

1. Using a yardstick and pencil, draw on the sheet a rectangle for the flag that measures 33¾ by 51 inches. This measurement allows for a 2-inch-deep hem all around with a ¼-inch-deep turn-under. Then draw another rectangle for the "stars" portion of the flag that measures 17½ by 24¾ inches. This allows for a 1-inch-deep hem all around plus a ¼-inch-deep turn-under. Cut out both rectangles with scissors.

2. Trace the star pattern on the tracing paper. Cut it out and glue it to the piece of cardboard; cut out the cardboard.

3. Making sure to allow enough extra fabric for the hem (see step 1), lay the star pattern in one corner of the smaller rectangle of cloth and lightly trace around it. Following the diagram for placement, trace around the star pattern forty-nine more times, arranging them in alternating vertical columns of four and five and separating them by about ½ inch.

ACTUAL SIZE

4. In the upper left-hand corner of the larger piece of fabric, mark off a rectangle measuring 15 by 22¼ inches—this area will be covered by the smaller "star" rectangle when the flag is assembled. Again, be sure to allow for the hem before drawing the rectangle. Now measure and pencil in the stripes after you have calculated for the hem. There should be thirteen stripes, each 2½ inches wide.

5. Place beeswax and paraffin in a ratio of about 4 parts to 6 parts in the metal can and set the can in the pan. Fill the pan with water and gently heat until the wax has melted. This "double-boiler" method is used to keep the wax, which is inflammable, away from the direct flames. Also, the hot water will keep the wax hot while you are using it. Last, it is a convenient method because the can is disposable. If the wax should happen to catch fire, throw baking soda on the flames.

6. When the wax is fully melted, test it to see whether it is ready for use: Use it to paint a star design on a scrap piece of cloth. If the wax soaks in, appears to be transparent for a few minutes, and does not run beyond the design edge, then it is ready to use.

7. Since the wax will soak through the cloth, cover the working surface with a thick layer of newspapers or newsprint paper. The cloth can be pulled away from the paper when the wax is dry. Place the rectangle

with the outlined stars on the newsprint and paint in the star shapes with wax. Be careful not to let the wax get too hot, even though it may seem easier to work with. Batik does not produce the neatest of products, but that is part of its handcrafted beauty. When the stars have been completed, turn the fabric over and wax the back of the stars, but this time do not let the cloth stick to the newsprint—pull it up each time you apply wax. When the star design is complete, put the fabric aside to dry.

8. Next, wax the front and back of the stripes that are to be white—that is, numbers 2, 4, 6, 8, 10, 12, following the directions given in step 7. Also wax the rectangle in the upper left-hand corner that will be covered by the star design, but wherever the unwaxed stripes touch the edge of this rectangle, leave 1 inch unwaxed. This is so that these stripes, which will be red, will "disappear" under the star-filled rectangle when it is stitched into position.

9. Mix the red and blue dyes in the two basins, following the manufacturer's directions.

10. Place the two waxed pieces of fabric in the freezer or other cold place for a few minutes to crisp-harden the wax for better "cracking." Remove from the freezer and crack all the wax with the exception of that on the rectangle in the upper left corner of the large piece. To crack the wax, squeeze the fabric with your hand for the desired effect.

11. Hold both pieces of fabric under cold running water to moisten. Put each one into the proper dye bath—the small "star" piece in the blue dye bath, the large one with the stripes in the red dye bath. When the right intensity of color has been obtained, remove the pieces from the bath and hang or lay them out to dry.

12. When the pieces are completely dry, place them between newspaper and iron them; each time the newspaper gets soaked with wax, replace it with fresh. Continue changing newspaper and ironing until no more wax shows through the paper.

13. Pin the hems on both pieces (see step 1), and press them into position. Pin the star piece to the upper left-hand corner of the striped rectangle, and sew it in place with clear nylon thread, using a blind stitch. Sew down the outside hem of the striped piece with clear nylon thread. (You can use a sewing machine for this step if you have one.)

14. Have the flag dry-cleaned to remove any remaining traces of wax.

10

Luau

In 1959, Hawaii officially became one of the United States on August 21, a good day for a luau. But you can have a Hawaiian luau in any warm summer month—indoors or out. The traditional Hawaiian one is held outside, featuring a deep pit dug in the earth large enough to roast a whole pig. Accompanying the roast pork are roasted or boiled tropical vegetables, fresh fruits piled high in baskets of palm leaves, and exotic leis strung around each guest's neck. Make a tiger lily and gardenia lei from our fabric flowers, or use the individual flowers to mark each guest's place at the feasting table. As a cool, crisp dessert for a hot night, serve our iced Hawaiian pineapple that has been dipped in chocolate.

TIGER LILIES

The following instructions are to make one flower, but make as many flowers as you need, carrying out each step in the multiples you will need for the number of flowers you are making. String the finished flowers together to make a lei, use them as place-setting markers, or arrange them in a huge bouquet for a lush, exotic centerpiece.

Tools and Materials

½ yard smooth-surfaced, no-iron polyester fabric: ¼ yard in orange (enough for two flowers) and ¼ yard in bright pink (enough for two flowers)
bath towel
white glue
soft, flat, artist's paintbrush, about 1 inch wide
covered wire, #36 and #20 gauge, in white
ruler
scissors
3 tubes acrylic paint: one each in pink, orange, and green
small, pointed, artist's paintbrush
1 slice white bread
india ink, in red
tracing paper, 8½ × 11 inches
paper towels
manila file folder or other lightweight cardboard
pencil
newspapers
felt-tipped marking pens: one each in red and orange
chalk or pastels: one each in light pink, dark pink, orange, and red
hair spray
satin ribbon, 1 inch wide, in olive green
masking tape
floral tape, in green

Instructions

1. Before beginning the project, "size," or stiffen, the fabric by spreading the material, right side down, over a bath towel spread flat on a table. Mix white glue with water and brush this mixture evenly over the back of the material. Hang up the material to dry. If you feel that the fabric is too wet, hold it in front of a hot radiator or a hot oven with the door open for a few minutes until partly dry.

2. To make the six stamens of the tiger lily, cut the #36-gauge wire into six 7½-inch lengths. Paint the wires with green acrylic paint and let dry. While the paint is drying, mix one crustless slice of white bread with 1 tablespoon of white glue, and mix until smooth. Form into six small, oval, berry-shaped stamen heads, each ⅜ inch long, and attach one to one end of each wire. Let dry until hard. When dough is dry, dip stamen heads into red india ink. With a paper towel, blot excess ink so that it will not run down the green wire. Set stamens to one side while you make the petals.

3. Trace the petal pattern, glue it to the file folder, and cut it out.

TIGER LILY PATTERN ACTUAL SIZE

4. Lay the pattern on the bias on the wrong side of the fabric and trace around it; then trace five more. Cut them out. To achieve a wavy, petallike edge, pull a bit on the edges with your fingers.

5. Now make the center vein for each petal. Cut the #20-gauge wire into six pieces, each one 7 inches long. Paint the wire with either pink or orange acrylic paint to match whichever color fabric you are using. When the wire is dry, lightly coat each piece with white glue and lay it down the center of the wrong side of a petal. The wire should extend 2 inches beyond one end of each petal. Let the glue on the petals dry before proceeding to the next step.

6. Next, add the characteristic tiger lily markings to the petals. Spread newspaper over a flat working surface. Place felt-tipped marking pens, colored chalk or pastels, and the hair spray in front of you and have paper towels handy to wipe off your fingers. With the red pen, draw a center line down each petal on the right side of the fabric, following the wire beneath the material. Blend in the pastel or chalk shades of light pink, dark pink, orange, and red along the surface of the petals. Now, lightly spray a petal with hair spray. Before the spray dries, quickly blend the color with a finger, smoothing one color into the other. Repeat this procedure with all the petals. When the petals are thoroughly dry, add a few red and orange dots, using the marking pens. (See the project photograph for the pattern of dots.)

7. To make the two leaves, cut the ribbon into two 5½- and two 3½-inch lengths. Also cut one 6-inch and one 4-inch length of the #20-gauge wire. Spread white glue on the wrong side of one long piece of ribbon, lay the 6-inch wire down the center the long way, and press the other long piece of ribbon, right side up, over the glue-covered ribbon and wire. The wire should extend ½ inch beyond one end. Place a weight over the leaf if necessary and allow to dry. Repeat this procedure with the remaining ribbon pieces and wire to make the smaller leaf. When the leaves are dry, taper each end to a long, curved point (see illustration).

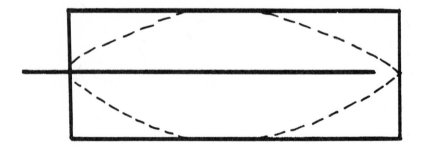

8. To assemble the flower, gather the six stamen wires in one hand. Add the six petals, wire extensions down, evenly around the cluster and hold them in place by twisting the extensions together. Twist the wire extensions of the two leaves around the other wires, and wrap all wire firmly together with masking tape; then cover the tape with green floral tape. Spread petals and stamens outward to make a loose, graceful flower form, and curve petals and leaves into a natural flower look.

GARDENIAS

All the materials needed in the making of the gardenias are duplicates of those listed for tiger lilies with the exception of those below, which are fabric and color substitutions. Many of the steps for the gardenias are also duplicates of those for the tiger lilies. Rather than repeat all instructions, references to step numbers will be made when appropriate.

Tools and Materials

½ yard velvet, in white (enough for four flowers)
2 tubes acrylic paint: one each in white and green
india ink, in yellow
felt-tipped marking pen, in dark green
¼ yard organdy, in green

Not Needed
polyester fabric
chalk or pastels
hair spray
satin ribbon

Instructions

1. "Size" the velvet (see step 1).
2. Make three stamens with 4-inch-long wires for each flower and three small teardrop-shaped stamen heads. Paint the wires green and, when the stamen heads are dry, dip them in yellow india ink. (See step 2.)
3. Trace the patterns for the three petals and leaf, glue them to the file folder, and cut them out. (See step 3.)
4. Trace five large petal shapes, four or five medium petal shapes,

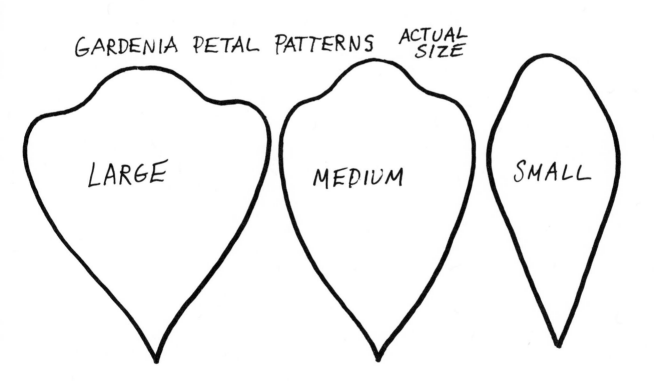

GARDENIA PETAL PATTERNS ACTUAL SIZE

LARGE

MEDIUM

SMALL

and three small petal shapes on the wrong side of the white velvet; cut out each petal with scissors. Cut #20-gauge wire into 5-inch lengths for each petal cut. Paint the wire with white acrylic paint. Glue wire to the underside of each petal, allowing at least 2 inches to extend from the base. (See step 5.)

5. Lay the leaf pattern on the green organdy and trace around it;

GARDENIA LEAF
PATTERN
ACTUAL
SIZE

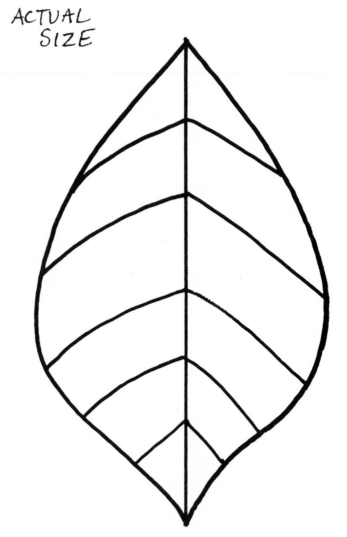

repeat three times. Cut out the four leaves. Cut four 7-inch lengths of the #20-gauge wire and paint them with the green acrylic paint. Glue each down the center of the underside of one leaf, allowing the wire to extend beyond one end. Weight the leaves and allow them to dry. Draw veins for the leaves on the right side of the fabric with the dark green marking pen as shown on pattern.

6. Now put the flower together. Start by twisting the lower wire portions of the three stamens together. Then twist the wires of the smaller petals together with the stamens. Next, wrap the wires of the medium petals around the center group. Finally add the larger petals, wrapping the wires around the center group of wires, each time arranging the petals around the center stamens. Add the four leaves at equal distances around the outer edge. Wrap all the wires tightly together with masking tape and then cover the masking tape with green floral tape.

7. Shape the petals and leaves into natural-looking forms.

FROZEN PINEAPPLE STICKS

Tools and Materials

1 medium, fresh pineapple cut into 1-inch chunks or 2 cans (20 ounces
   each) canned pineapple chunks
bamboo or metal skewers or chopsticks
1½ cups chopped walnuts
1 pound or more milk chocolate bars
heavy saucepan
fork or whisk
small ladle

Instructions

1. At least a day before you wish to serve these, skewer the pineapple chunks and freeze them. Make sure that they are completely frozen before proceeding with this project. (*Note:* Frozen pineapple chunks will keep in the freezer for as long as a month or two, so if you make them ahead, you can easily serve them on the spur of the moment.)
2. Pour the walnuts over the bottom of a dinner plate.
3. Using a deep, narrow, heavy saucepan, melt the milk chocolate over a pan of boiling water, stirring occasionally until all the chocolate is melted. Blend thoroughly with a fork or whisk.
4. Set the pan of chocolate, still over the hot water, in the center of a working surface. Then put the chopped walnuts on one side and the frozen pineapple on the other side. Working over the pan, ladle the melted chocolate over each frozen pineapple kebab. The chocolate will begin to set as soon as it touches the frozen pineapple, so work quickly.
5. As each kebab is coated with chocolate, immediately roll it in the chopped walnuts. Again, you must work very quickly or the chocolate will harden and the nuts won't adhere.
6. Serve immediately or keep in the freezer until ready to serve.

11

Mexican Independence Day

In September, the Mexicans celebrate their Independence Day, which makes September a good time for us to have a celebration, too—with a South-of-the-border feast. Start the party off, as the Mexicans do, with a pinata, a papier-mâché pig, in this case, filled with small goodies—wrapped candies, nuts, and tiny gifts. Hang the pinata from the ceiling, blindfold a guest at a time, give him a stick, and let him take one whack in the direction of the pig. Finally, one of the guests will whack on target, break the pig, and spill out its goodies all over the floor. Then it's time for everyone to share in the loot. Add some of our small clay figures to the pinata, use them as place decorations, march them around the centerpiece of the table, or string them on a thong for a necklace. The vibrant chili pepper necklace, also made of clay, will add spice to any outfit on any occasion.

A PINATA PIG

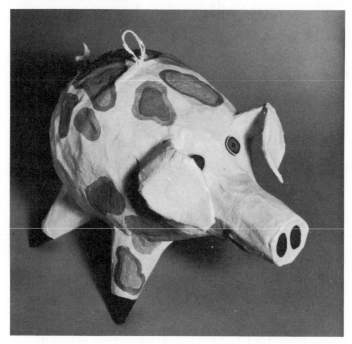

If you would like to keep your pinata, cut a slot in the top before painting it and use it as a giant piggy bank.

Tools and Materials

large, oval balloon, approximately 6½ inches long × 10 inches around
  when blown up
string or twine
Celluclay (packaged papier-mâché)
flour
white glue
newspaper
1 piece aluminum foil, 5 × 6 inches
1 paper cup, 8-ounce size
lightweight cardboard or manila folders
scissors
transparent tape
1 piece uncorrugated cardboard, about 8½ × 11 inches
three or four pipe cleaners
gesso
artist's paintbrushes
masking tape
wrapped candies and trinkets (for filling pinata)
4 tubes acrylic paints: one each in chrome yellow, cerise, green, and
  bright blue
2 square buttons, each about ¾ inch in diameter, in blue

Instructions

1. Blow up balloon to size specified in materials list; fasten securely.

2. Wrap string or twine several times around the balloon 5 inches in from each end, using some of the twine to fashion a generous loop for hanging up the finished pinata.

3. Mix Celluclay according to the manufacturer's directions. Also mix some flour with water to make a thin paste; add some white glue. Tear newspaper into strips about an inch wide.

4. Begin forming the pig's body by covering the balloon with the Celluclay. Cover the whole surface with a coat about ⅛ inch thick *except* for a 3- by 4-inch rectangle on the top of the body near one

end—this end will become the rear of the body. The opening will be used for filling the pinata just before the final painting of the outside surface. A cover will then be fitted into place and the cracks covered with Celluclay.

5. To make the cover, fit the piece of aluminum foil into the uncovered top area of the balloon. Turn up the extra 1 inch all around to form walls. Fill in the area with ⅛ inch of Celluclay and let dry.

TIN FOIL

6. When the Celluclay is dry on both body and cover, continue to build up the surface of the pig and the cover until both are about ½ inch thick. Build about ⅛ inch at a time, keeping the surface as smooth as possible and allowing time to dry before proceeding.

7. Cover both body and cover with a few layers of crisscrossed newspaper strips. Before laying the strips, pull them through the flour-and-water paste.

8. To make the snout, cover the outside of the paper cup with Celluclay or newspaper strips dipped in the flour-and-water paste; let dry.

9. Using lightweight cardboard, form four cones that are 3½ inches long each—these will become the legs. Hold them together with strips of tape and then cover them with either Celluclay or newspaper strips dipped in the flour-and-water paste; let dry.

10. Cut out two ear shapes from the cardboard, following the diagram for the correct measurements. Cover each ear except for the

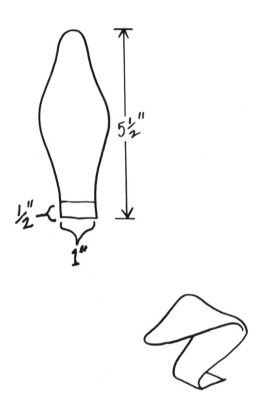

½-inch-wide flap with Celluclay. Bend the ears into position while still wet; then let dry.

11. Loosely twist a few pipe cleaners together to form a corkscrew tail; cover it with Celluclay.

12. Let all the pieces dry thoroughly. Lift off the cover by the edges of the exposed aluminum foil and set to one side. Next attach snout,

legs, ears, and tail with white glue. When the glue has dried, cover all the joining areas with Celluclay and then newspaper strips dipped in flour-and-water paste, smoothing out the body so that all the seams are hidden. Let dry.

13. Now add the smooth surface coat. Starting with the legs, paint the entire pig with gesso, which will dry to a smooth, white surface. Also coat the cover with gesso. Let both pieces dry until hard.

14. Prick the balloon at the opening and cut away any rubber showing. Fill pig with candy and trinkets, but do not fill it so full that it is too heavy to stand on its legs. Cover the opening from the inside with masking tape, sticky side up. Cover the sides of the opening and the sides of the cover with white glue. Set the cover in place over the masking tape and press down lightly. Squeeze white glue around the crack, and let dry. Fill crack with Celluclay, smooth over lightly, and cover crack with strips of newspaper pulled through flour-and-water paste. Let dry, and then cover the joining area with a light brushing of gesso.

15. When all is dry, paint the entire body with the yellow paint; let dry. Then paint large, random spots on the body with cerise and green. When dry, broadly outline the cerise spots with green and the green with cerise. Paint in two nostrils, a smiling mouth, and the feet with the blue paint.

16. With white glue, attach the buttons to make the eyes.

OVEN-BAKED CLAY JEWELRY

Although we show our flowers and animals standing, they're actually beads ready for stringing into a necklace. Of course, you can use them in other ways, too, such as table decorations.

Tools and Materials

oven-baked clay, such as Sculpture House's Della Robbia or Stewart Clay Company's Ceraclay (available at art-supply stores or by mail order)
small sponge (for smoothing clay)
small, pointed knife (for forming clay)
clay-working tools (optional)
small baking skewer
baking sheet
7 tubes acrylic paints: one each in blue, brown, green, orange, red, white, and yellow
fine-pointed artist's paintbrushes
heavy nylon bead-stringing thread, twine, or leather thongs

Instructions

1. Following the manufacturer's directions for working and forming the clay, form the shapes you wish for your necklace (see steps 4 through 6 for specific instructions for making each necklace). When the shapes are almost dry, punch a small hole with a skewer through each so that it can be strung with nylon thread, twine, or leather thongs when finished. Then place the shapes on the baking sheet and bake according to manufacturer's directions. Either clay will bake in a hour or two.
2. When the clay shapes are cool, paint them with acrylic paints.
3. String the shapes on the stringing materials and tie the ends together. The necklaces should be long enough to go over the head, even though the decorative area will be only in the front from just below each shoulder.

4. To make the chili pepper necklace, form six pepper shapes, each about 2 inches long and ⅝ inch wide at its thickest point. Then make eight leaves, each 1 to 1¼ inches long and ¾ to ⅞ inch wide. Paint the peppers a clear, bright red blending into an orange-red, with a green calyx and stem. Paint the leaves a medium green with dark green veins. String the peppers and leaves so that there are two leaves between the center four peppers and one leaf between the others.
5. To make the clay figures for one necklace, follow the assembling

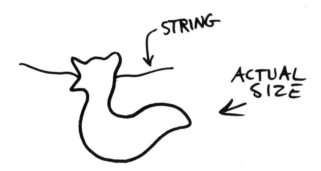

diagrams and the project photograph to construct a duck shape; eight spheres, each ½ inch in diameter; and four 4-legged animal shapes—one to resemble a horse, one a lamb, one a bull, and one a cow. Paint the duck white with red spots, the spheres bright blue, the horse blue with red, yellow, and green designs, the lamb white with

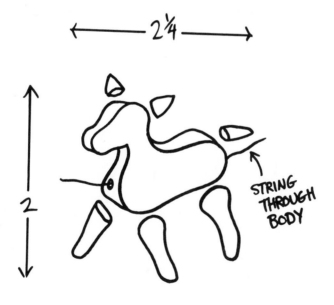

red and green decorations, the bull red brown with yellow, green, and blue decorations, and the cow white. String two of the spheres on a length of stringing material, add an animal, then a sphere, and con-

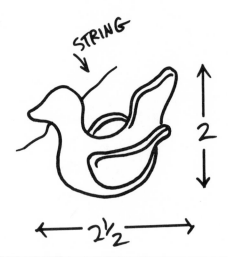

STRING

2

2½

tinue stringing in this pattern with the remaining shapes, ending with two spheres.

6. To make a bird and flower necklace, follow the diagrams and photograph to construct three ducks (step 5), four birds, and four 5-petaled flower shapes. Paint the flowers bright blue; paint the birds and flowers in bright colors of blue, yellow, orange, red, and green. When stringing the objects, intersperse the birds with the flower shapes.

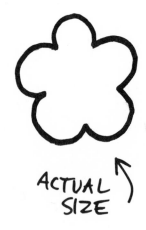

ACTUAL SIZE

12

Halloween

On All Hallow's Eve, traditionally the night before the day to mourn the dead, ghosts walked, skeletons rose from their graves, witches swirled through the sky on their broomsticks creating mischief, turning milk sour, rattling doors and windows—and the whole night was filled with strange happenings. Many of our customs for celebrating Halloween—jack-o'-lanterns and trick-or-treating—came from Ireland during the middle of the last century. In turn, children today dress as ghosts and witches and hide their faces behind masks while they collect their treats from house to house.

Here is a demon mask that is guaranteed to frighten away any strange spirit abroad on this night, and the gleaming jack-o'-lanterns will protect the house from evil spirits as their lights alternately quiver and steadfastly shine from a window, lighting the way for the trick-or-treaters. The lollibugs, with their clear, bright colors and tasty hard candy perched on a lollipop stick, are treats guaranteed to prevent tricks.

DEMON MASK

Tools and Materials

ruler
pencil
brown wrapping paper
1 sheet posterboard, 9 × 12 inches, in light orange
6 sheets medium-weight construction paper, each 9 × 12 inches: one
    each in black, purple, white, dark green, light green, and red orange
scissors
#1 X-acto knife with #11 blades
white glue
permanent felt-tipped marking pen, in black
elastic thread, in black
stapler

Instructions

1. Using the ruler and pencil on brown wrapping paper, enlarge all

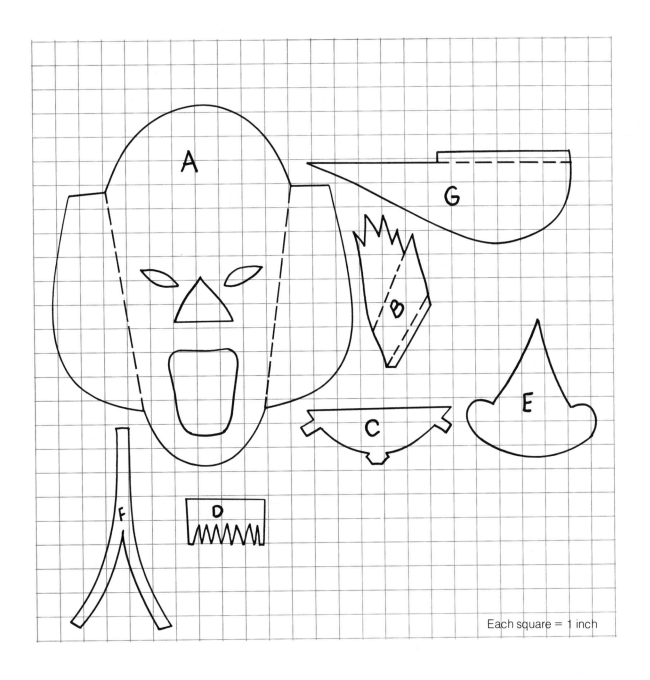

Each square = 1 inch

the pattern pieces by the grid method. Cut out the pieces, label them, and transfer all pattern markings, such as dotted lines.

2. Lay pattern A on the back of the orange posterboard and, while holding it firmly in place, trace around the pattern with a pencil. With the scissors, cut out the face along the outside line. Working on a wooden cutting surface and using the X-acto knife, cut out the eyes, nose, and mouth; hold the knife as you would a pencil, draw it toward yourself to cut, and press firmly enough to cut cleanly through the posterboard with just one stroke. Next position the ruler so that one edge runs along one of the dotted lines. Holding the ruler in place with one hand, score the board by lightly running the blade of the X-acto knife along the edge of the ruler. Be very careful not to cut too deeply.

129

Repeat to cut along the other dotted line. Then bend the side sections back along the scored lines.

3. With the pencil, outline pattern B (eyelash) on the black construction paper. Turn the pattern over so that the shape will be in reverse and outline a second eyelash. Transfer the dotted lines on the pattern piece to both eyelashes and, using the scissors, cut out the pieces. Laying the ruler along each dotted line, fold the eyelashes as shown in the illustration.

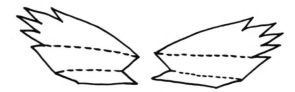

Using the X-acto knife, cut slits in the bottom section of each eyelash, as shown in the illustration.

These slits will enable you to curve the eyelashes to lie along the contours of the eyes. Dab white glue on the back of each tab, curve the shape to correspond to the upper part of the eye opening, as shown in the illustration, and press it in place.

Hold the tabs in place until the glue has set. Repeat the same procedure to attach the second eyelash.

4. Outline pattern C (mouth) twice on the purple construction paper and cut out both pieces. Fold the tabs up. Place a small amount of white glue on the center tabs of both pieces and position them as shown in the illustration.

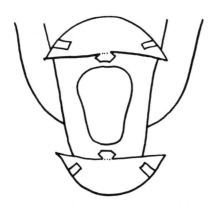

Next, place glue on the backs of the two remaining tabs of the upper lip. Bend the lip section toward the mouth and hold the glued side of the tabs against the orange posterboard, as shown in the illustration, until the glue has set.

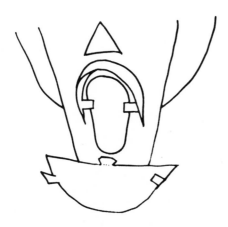

Repeat to add the lower lip. Then, using the X-acto knife, cut away the sections of tabs that extend into the open mouth.

5. Outline pattern D (teeth) twice on the white construction paper and cut out both pieces. Place small dots of glue on the areas indicated by X's on the pattern and press them in place, as shown in the illustration.

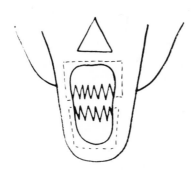

6. Outline pattern E (nose) on the dark green construction paper and cut it out. Place dots of glue on the back of the nose in the places

indicated by X's on the pattern piece. Press the nose onto the orange posterboard, as shown in the illustration, and hold it there until the glue has set.

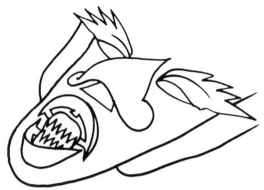

7. Outline pattern F (eyebrow) on the light green construction paper and cut it out. Place a small amount of glue on the front of the two lower ends and press these sections against the backs of the eyelashes, as shown in the illustration. Hold them in place until the glue has set.

Place a small amount of glue on the back of the eyebrow at the top, pull the piece so that it's taut, and bend the top of the piece around to the back of the orange posterboard, as shown in the illustration. Hold it in place until the glue has set.

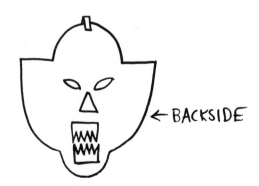

← BACKSIDE

8. Outline pattern G (ear) on the red orange construction paper. Turn the pattern over so that the shape will be in reverse and trace a second ear. Transfer the dotted lines, and cut out both pieces. Bend both tabs toward the back of the ears along the dotted line. Squeeze small dots of glue along the tabs and press them into place on the side sections of the orange posterboard, as shown in the illustration.

Hold the ears in place until the glue has set.
9. Using the marking pen, color in the tabs inside the mouth area.
10. Cut two lengths of elastic thread (the exact length needed will depend on the head size of the person wearing the mask). Tie knots at each end of the two lengths, and staple one end to each side of the mask, as shown in the illustration.

BACKSIDE

Tools and Materials

ruler
pencil
3 manila file folders or other lightweight cardboard
scissors
3 pumpkins
grease pencil, in black
apple corer
#6 X-acto knife with a whittling blade or a thin, sharp paring knife
short votive candles

Instructions

1. Using the ruler and pencil on the file folders, enlarge the three designs by the grid method.

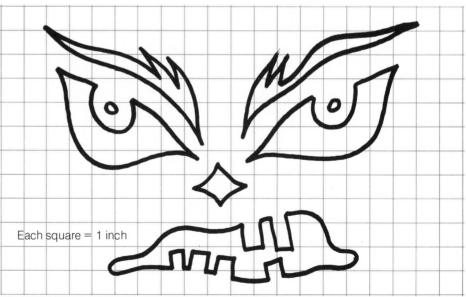

Each square = 1 inch

Each square = 1 inch

Cut out each of the features with scissors.

2. Cut open the tops of the pumpkins with the X-acto knife to make lids and remove seeds and the pulp immediately around the seeds. If the walls are exceedingly thick, thin the area where the faces will be cut by scraping them with a spoon.

3. Position one of the cardboard patterns on one of the pumpkins, and lightly trace around the features with a grease pencil. You can shift the pattern to accommodate the features to the particular shape of your pumpkin. Repeat the procedure with the other two patterns and pumpkins.

135

4. Using the apple corer, punch out the pupils in the eyes. Next use the X-acto blade or sharp, pointed knife to cut around the iris of the eyes. To achieve this curve, first make a series of tiny, straight cuts that form a circle; then make the final cut. Any severe curve must be cut this way.

5. Cut out all the remaining features with the knife, working in short sawing motions with a sharp blade. Pumpkins cut very easily, so avoid putting too much pressure on the blade or it may shoot off in the wrong direction.

6. When all the features have been cut, use the end of a large spoon to punch out the pieces. Use a damp cloth to remove the grease pencil marks.

7. Place a candle inside each pumpkin and light it.

LOLLIBUGS

Because the syrup to make the lollibugs is extremely hot, do not let children pour out the shapes – let them instead put together the shapes with the colors they like, assembling the lollibugs. The cooked syrup is an amber color, so that blue food coloring will turn very dull; use other colors for best results.

Tools and Materials

ruler
pencil
tracing paper, 8½ × 11 inches
aluminum foil
candy thermometer
pastry brush
Lollipop Mixture (recipe follows)
wooden popsicle sticks

137

Instructions

1. With pencil on the tracing paper, trace all lollibug shapes.
2. Spread large sheets of aluminum foil over a working surface and lay the pattern pieces on top. Trace over the lines with a sharp pencil to impress light lines in the foil to use as a guide in pouring the hot syrup shapes.
3. Prepare the Lollipop Mixture:

LOLLIPOP MIXTURE
2 cups sugar
¾ cup light corn syrup
½ cup water
½ teaspoon any flavoring desired (optional)
food coloring, in color(s) of your choice

In a deep, heavy saucepan, mix sugar, corn syrup, and water. Stir over medium heat until the sugar dissolves. Boil without stirring until the temperature on a candy thermometer reaches 310 degrees F. or until drops of syrup form hard, brittle threads in cold water. While syrup is boiling, wash down any sugar crystals clinging to the sides of the pan with a pastry brush dipped in cold water. Remove from the heat and stir in desired flavoring and coloring. If you wish to work with more than one color, pour out the amount you wish for the first color and add the food coloring; place the remainder of the batch over a pan of boiling water until you are ready to use it.
4. Working with one batch of lollipop mixture at a time and pouring out scant amounts of syrup so that the completed lollibugs will not be too heavy to pick up on a stick, pour out wings, heads, and eyes onto the aluminum foil, pouring at least twice as many wing shapes as heads—you may want to use as many as six wings per lollibug. You will also need twice as many eye shapes as heads. Use a spoon to spread the wing shapes into points. Then pour several body shapes and immediately press a lollipop stick into each before it hardens.
5. Using a batch of another color, pour out more wing shapes, heads, and eyes. Again, pour out a few body shapes and press sticks into them. Continue pouring as many shapes of different colors as you wish.
6. Release all shapes by peeling away the aluminum foil.
7. "Glue" the wings, heads, and eyes to the bodies with clear or colored lollipop syrup by dipping the contact side of wings, head, and eyes in the syrup and quickly pressing them to the body. To add interest, combine several colors in each lollibug. To add stripes, mouths, and eyeballs, use a spoon to drizzle small amounts of colored syrup on the hardened bodies in the shapes you want.

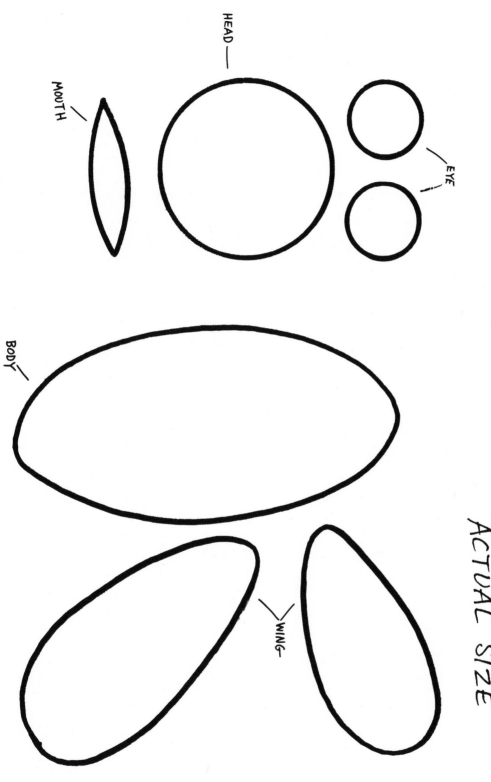

MOUTH

HEAD

EYE

BODY

WING

LOLLIBUG PATTERNS
ACTUAL SIZE

13

Harvest Day

Harvest Day is part of the farming world all around the globe, celebrating the feeling of accomplishment and satisfaction that wells up when the crops are in and stored away for the long winter ahead. It is a time of full moons, hayrides, and crisp air spiced with the smell of burning leaves. In times past, when the corn was being husked, dolls—whole families with mothers, fathers, and children—were fashioned of the dried husks to last through the winter playtime. They have a quaint charm now, but they are still cherished as playmates or as decorations for a harvest table. Our wooden truck is as much a part of our modern farm as the doll is of the old-fashioned one. The truck here holds a sample of the produce brought into the market and of the good things available at the harvest feast—for which it can serve as a centerpiece. Afterward, it will make a delightful toy to keep a youngster occupied during the cold rains of winter.

CORN HUSK DOLL

Tools and Materials

dried corn husks
ruler
straight pins
pipe cleaner, 6 inches long, in white
string
white glue
dried cornsilk
small, tinted dried flowers or 1 square of fabric, 2 × 2 inches, needle, thread, and 3 to 4 inches ribbon, ⅛ to ¼ inch wide
caraway, dill, and sesame seeds; split peas; lentils; raw rice; peppercorns
felt-tipped marking pen, in black (optional)

Instructions

Doll

1. Soak dried corn husks in warm water for 5 to 10 minutes. Always work with wet corn husks, remoistening them when needed.
2. To form the head, tear some of the husks into ¼-inch-wide strips and roll them into a ¾-inch-diameter ball. Use straight pins to hold the husks in place.
3. Following step 2, make a 1-inch-diameter ball for the upper body.
4. To make arms, place a pipe cleaner in the center of a 1-inch-wide strip of husk and wrap the husk around the pipe cleaner so that the pipe cleaner is covered. Tie each end with string. To form sleeves, cut two 9-inch-long pieces from the thick ends of two corn husks and tie them ¼ inch in from each end of the covered pipe cleaner, leaving about 1½ inches overlapping each end. Then fold each end of the

husks back toward the middle of the arms and tie them with a ⅛-inch-wide strip of corn husk; trim away excess.

5. To cover the ball for the head, drape a 1-inch-wide husk smoothly over the ball, twist the excess husk to make the "neck," and trim the ends so that about 3 to 3½ inches hang below the head. Tie a string

firmly around the "neck" to hold it in place. The covered parts of the ball will become the face and the back of the head. The ends of the husks will hold the body to the head.

6. Place a drop of white glue on top of the body ball and drape the arm piece over it, securing the arm piece with a straight pin.

7. Put a drop of white glue on top of the body-ball, and press the head, with the hanging ends at the front and back of the body, against this glue. Cover the ball with the ends of the husks hanging from the head, twisting and tying them with string at the "waist," which is the bottom of the body-ball. The skirt will be formed around the hanging ends.

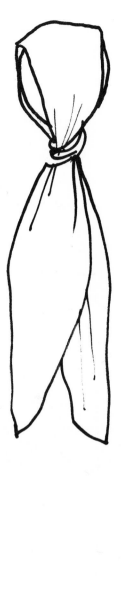

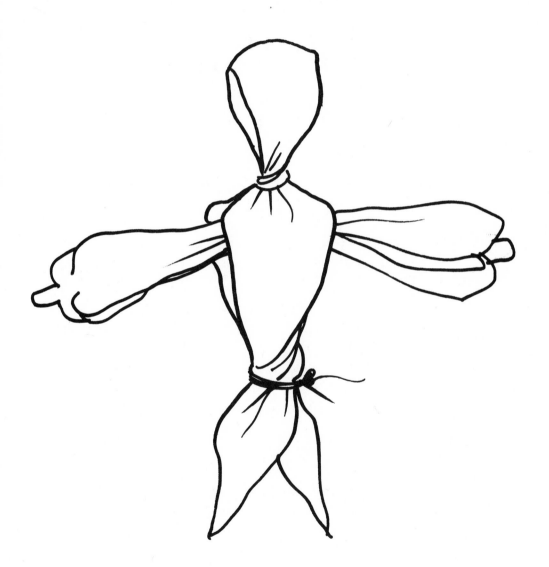

8. Next, make the skirt by overlapping the narrow ends of a number of husks around the waist so that the convex curve of the husk is on the outside. Use your judgment about how wide the husks should be. Use

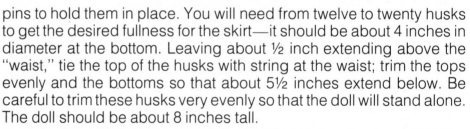

pins to hold them in place. You will need from twelve to twenty husks to get the desired fullness for the skirt—it should be about 4 inches in diameter at the bottom. Leaving about ½ inch extending above the "waist," tie the top of the husks with string at the waist; trim the tops evenly and the bottoms so that about 5½ inches extend below. Be careful to trim these husks very evenly so that the doll will stand alone. The doll should be about 8 inches tall.

9. Make the shawl-blouse next. Cut a thin V into a husk, ending the shape halfway up the husk. Holding the uncut portion at the back of

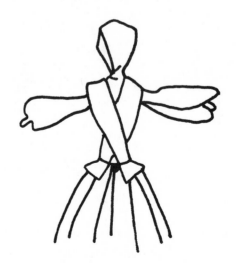

the waist, pull each half up and around the shoulders to the front, cross the ends, and tie the front and the back of the shawl-blouse with string at the waist to secure it. Cover the string ties with a strip of husk ¼ to ⅜ inch wide and tie it in back.

10. Soak cornsilk in water for 5 minutes. Make two braids and use pins to attach them to the head for the hair. Fray the top edges to form hair over the top of the head.

11. Glue small dried flowers around the head to form a wreath or make a bonnet for it from the fabric square as follows: Cut a small circle out of the fabric piece, and sew a row of small running stitches ⅛ inch in

from the edge. Put over head and pull on one end of the thread to gather the fabric to fit the head. Fasten off the thread. Tie a piece of bright ribbon around the bonnet to cover the stitches.

12. Let the doll dry overnight. Then remove any obvious pins, but leave in those needed to hold corn husks in place.

13. Decorate doll and her clothing as desired, forming small patterns with rice; split peas; lentils; caraway, dill, and sesame seeds; and peppercorns.

14. Glue caraway seeds to the face to make features or draw them in with a black, felt-tipped pen.

Small Basket

15. Cut the stiff ends of several husks into six strips, each ¼ inch wide and approximately 7 inches long. Bend each into a U shape, making the bottom of the U approximately 1½ inches wide. Let dry.

16. Crisscross the U's and hold them in position with a straight pin thrust through the center of all the husks.

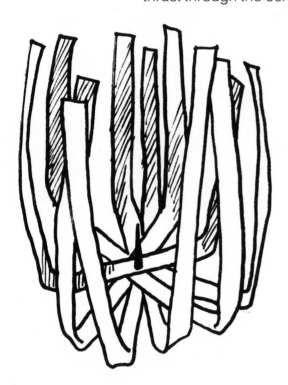

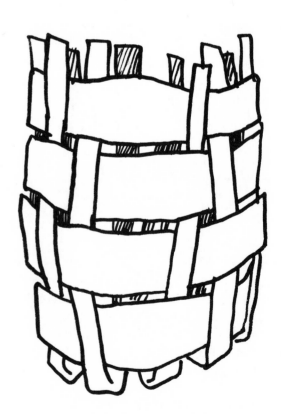

17. Weave four strips of husks, each ¼ to ½ inch wide, through the crisscrossed U's to hold the sides together.

18. Turn the tops of the U strips to the inside of the basket and hold them in place with pins and white glue.

19. Twist a 5-inch length of husk into a "rope" for a handle. Attach the handle to opposite sides of the basket with pins and white glue. Let the basket dry, and then remove excess pins. Fill the basket with dried flowers.

Large Basket

20. Make the larger basket in the same way, but increase the size of the husks you use.

WOODEN PRODUCE TRUCK CENTERPIECE

Tools and Materials

1 piece plywood, ¼ inch thick × 8 inches wide × 15 inches long
1 piece plywood, ¾ inch thick × 13 inches wide × 13½ inches long
1 piece pine lattice, ¼ inch thick × 1 inch wide × 8 feet long
wooden doweling: 7 inches of ⅛-inch-diameter and 10 inches of
    5/16-inch-diameter
coping saw
assorted hand saws
white glue
small finishing nails
hammer
assorted wood rasps
fine sandpaper
clear varnish or lacquer
paintbrushes (for wood stain and varnish)
brace or electric drill with ⅛-inch and 5/16-inch bits
wood stain, in walnut or other dark color

Instructions

1. Saw out all the pieces needed for the truck, following the pattern drawings for shapes, sizes, wood types, and wood thicknesses.

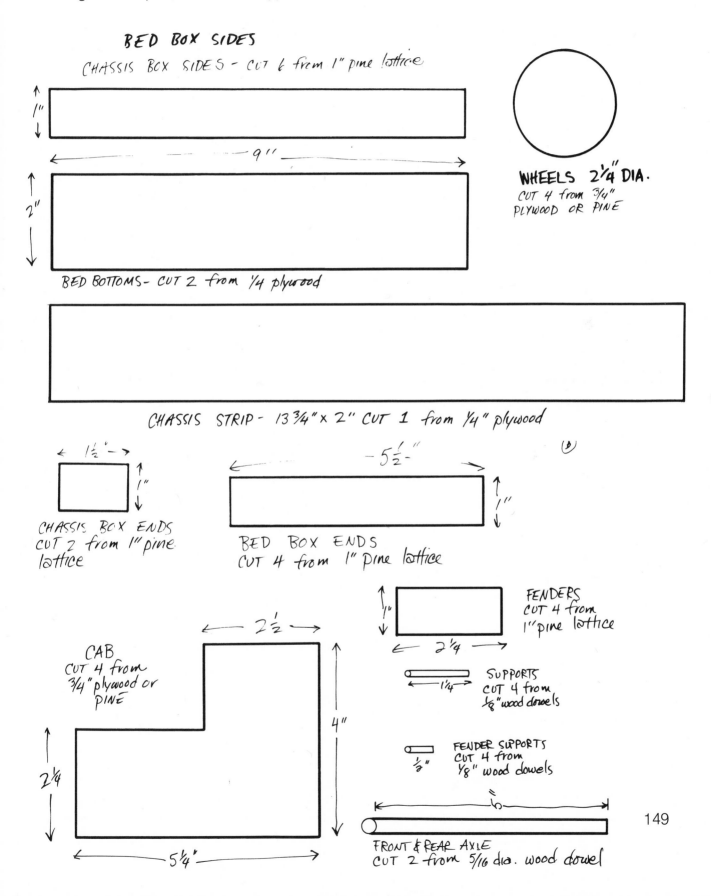

BED BOX SIDES

CHASSIS BOX SIDES - CUT 6 from 1" pine lattice

1"

9"

2"

BED BOTTOMS- CUT 2 from 1/4 plywood

WHEELS 2 1/4" DIA.
CUT 4 from 3/4"
PLYWOOD OR PINE

CHASSIS STRIP- 13 3/4" x 2" CUT 1 from 1/4" plywood

1 1/2"

1"

CHASSIS BOX ENDS
CUT 2 from 1" pine
lattice

5 1/2"

1"

BED BOX ENDS
CUT 4 from 1" pine lattice

FENDERS
CUT 4 from
1" pine lattice

1"

2 1/4

SUPPORTS
CUT 4 from
1/8" wood dowels

1 1/4

CAB
CUT 4 from
3/4" plywood or
PINE

2 1/2

4"

FENDER SUPPORTS
CUT 4 from
1/8" wood dowels

1/2"

2 1/4

5 1/4"

FRONT & REAR AXLE
CUT 2 from 5/16 dia. wood dowel

2. Glue and nail together the four cab sections, following the diagram.

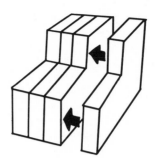

When the glue is dry, sand the rough wood smooth and slightly curve all edges with a wood rasp; varnish and let dry.
3. Using the 5/16-inch bit, drill halfway through the center of one side of each wheel—the axle will be fitted into this hole. Sand and varnish the sides of the wheels; stain the edges. Let dry.
4. Sand the rough areas of the five chassis pieces and slightly round the edges with the wood rasp. Stain all pieces. Glue and nail together the chassis-box sides and ends. Varnish the ends and sides and let dry; varnish the long chassis strip.

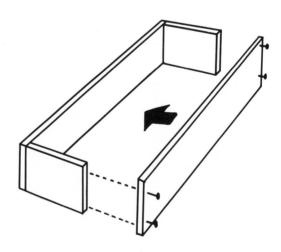

5. While the chassis box and chassis strip are drying, construct two bed boxes. Glue and nail the sides and ends together and then nail both bottom pieces to one of the two units, as shown in the diagram.

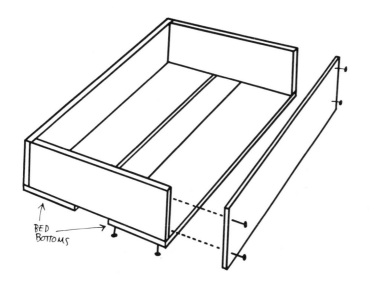

Sand the wood smooth, slightly curve the edges with the wood rasp, stain, and varnish; let dry.

6. Glue and nail the three sections together—the chassis strip, the chassis box, and the solid-bottomed bed box—as shown in the diagram. Line up the pieces so that the rear sections are flush.

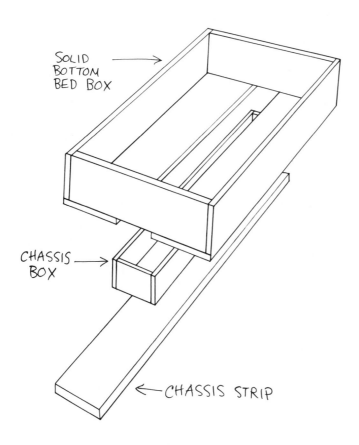

7. Glue and nail the cab to the bed box and chassis, centering the cab on the chassis, as shown.

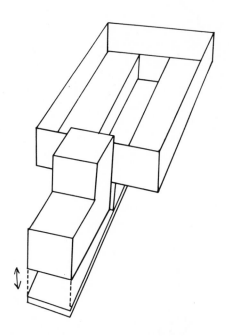

8. Cut the 5/16-inch dowel into two lengths, each 5 inches long. Place a wheel on the end of each rod to make two axles.
9. Nail the axles to the chassis, as shown. The front axle should be 1½

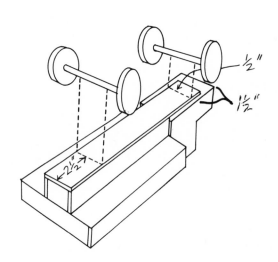

inches in from the front of the cab; the rear axle should be 2½ inches in from the rear of the chassis-box.
10. Using the ⅛-inch bit, drill four matching holes, each ⅜ inch deep,

Wooden Produce Truck Centerpiece

Corn Husk Doll

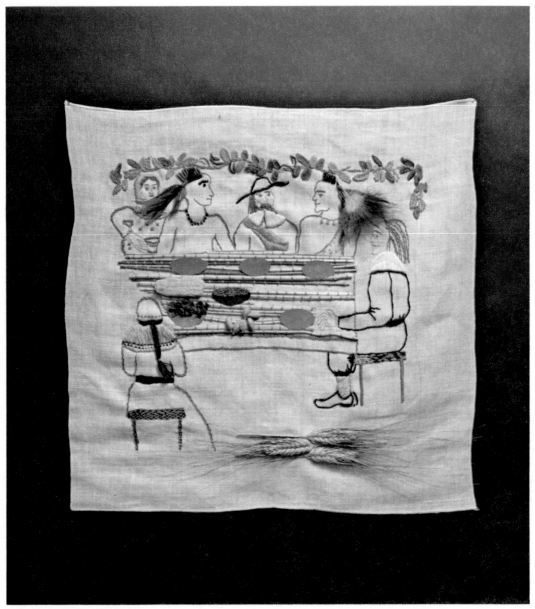
Embroidering the First Thanksgiving

Demon Mask

Jack-O'Lanterns

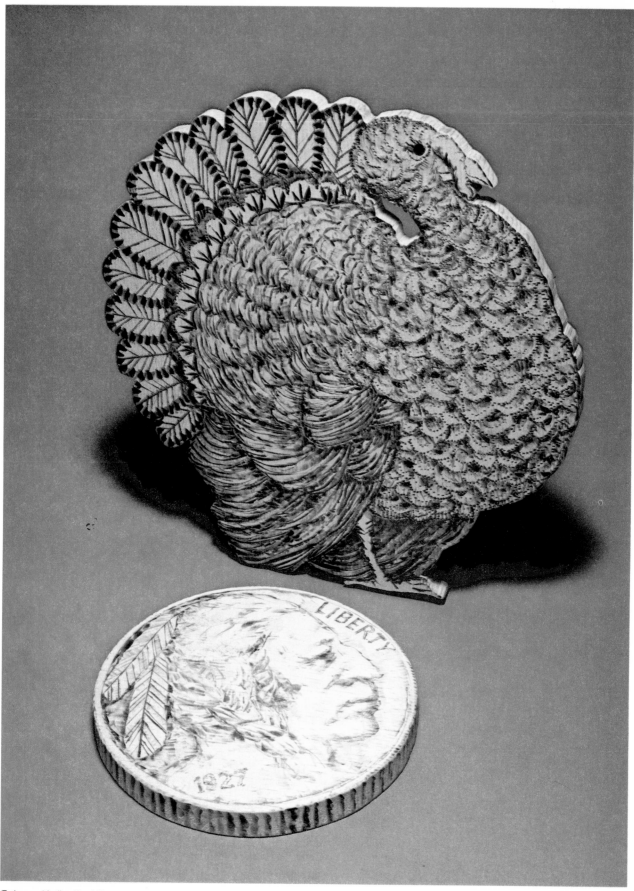

Turkey and Indian Head Hotpads

Lollibugs

Cornucopia with Cream Puffs

into the thickness of the front and back ends of the two bed boxes, as shown. Cut the ⅛-inch dowel into four 1¼-inch-long pieces for sup-

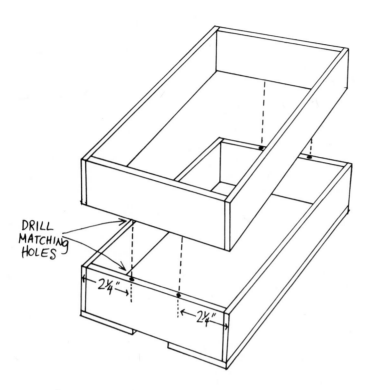

ports between the bed boxes. Glue a dowel in each hole of the bottom bed box and then glue the other ends into the matching holes of the top bed box. The top bed box should now be lined up with the top of the cab.

11. Cut a 45-degree angle on one end of two of the fender pieces, as shown in the diagram. Cut the ⅛-inch dowel into four ½-inch lengths.

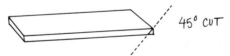

Using the ⅛-inch bit, center and drill a ⅛-inch-deep hole through each of the four fender pieces and glue a dowel into each. Then apply stain and varnish. Glue together the two fenders, using one fender piece with straight edges and one with an angled edge for each fender.

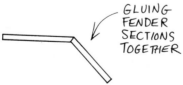

12. Set a complete fender on top of one of the front wheels and mark on the wheel where the two dowels touch. In those spots, drill a ⅛-inch-deep hole, still using the ⅛-inch bit. Repeat on other wheels. Glue the fender dowels into the wheels.

14

Thanksgiving

Thanksgiving Day at the end of November was the Pilgrims' harvest day, a day of showing gratitude for having survived a rigorous life in a new land, far away from the civilized world they knew. The wooden turkey and Indian head hotpads are reminders of that first feast—the turkey that was the center of the feast and the Indian who helped the Pilgrims through their hard times, teaching them the survival skills in a new environment. Your own turkey platter and dish of hot succotash can rest proudly on these wooden supports. The whole Pilgrim legend is celebrated in the modern embroidered picture incorporating bits of wheat, seeds, and feathers into a design that shows Pilgrims and Indians at that first celebration. From ancient times, cornucopias have been a symbol of plenty; our puff-paste cornucopia spills out whipped-cream-filled puffs as a bountiful dessert for your feast of Thanksgiving.

TURKEY HOTPAD

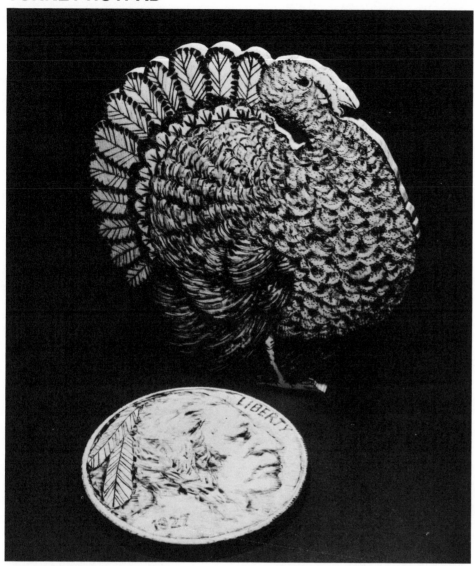

Tools and Materials

medium sandpaper
1 piece pine, ¾ inch thick × 13 inches wide × 14 inches long
ruler
hard pencil
1 sheet drawing paper, 18 × 24 inches
4 sheets carbon paper, each 8½ × 11½ inches
masking tape
jigsaw
hand or electric drill with ⅜-inch-diameter bit
woodburning tool with tip

Instructions

1. If necessary, smooth the top and bottom surfaces of the pine with sandpaper.

2. Using the ruler and pencil on the drawing paper, enlarge the turkey pattern by the grid method.

Each square = 1 inch

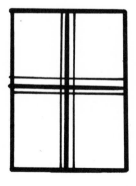

3. Lay the four sheets of carbon paper next to each other as shown in the diagram. Turn them so that the carbon sides all face the same way and tape all the edges together to make one large piece. Place the piece, carbon side down, over the better side of the wood and lay the pattern, design side up, on top. Trace over the outline and design lines with the pencil to transfer it to the wood; carefully remove the pattern and carbon paper.

4. Cut around the outer edge of the design with a jigsaw. Then drill a hole in the negative area behind the turkey's neck, insert the jigsaw, and finish cutting out this center piece.

5. Smooth all cut edges with sandpaper.

6. Practice using the woodburning tool on a piece of scrap wood, noting that the tip and straight edge of the tool will burn thin, dark lines. The sides of the burner, when quickly run over the wood, will burn areas that are light in tone. When you are ready to begin woodburning the project, trace over all the dark lines first; do the shaded areas last.

INDIAN HEAD NICKLE HOTPAD

To make the Indian head nickle, you will need the same tools and materials that are listed for the turkey hotpad except for the drill. A few of the items should be of a different size or quantity; these changes are listed below. Then simply follow the instructions given for the turkey, substituting the Indian head design and omitting step 4.

Tools and Materials

1 piece pine, ¾ inch thick × 8 inches wide × 8 inches long
1 sheet drawing paper, 9 × 9 inches, in white
2 sheets carbon paper, each 8½ × 11½ inches

Each square = 1 inch

EMBROIDERING THE FIRST THANKSGIVING

Tools and Materials

4 sheets tracing paper, each 8½ × 11 inches
transparent tape
ruler
soft pencil
linen napkin with finished edge, 16½ × 17 inches, in white
embroidery thread, in tan, white, brown, yellow, black, rust, orange,
    and six shades of green
package of embroidery needles
scissors
embroidery hoop
feathers (available from craft-supply stores)
needle
thread
dried wheat heads and stalks
gauze
sandpaper
acrylic matte medium, such as Liquitex
dried beans
cardamom seeds

Instructions

1. Tape together the four sheets of tracing paper to make a rectangle
17 × 22 inches and enlarge the design on it by the grid method. Then,

Each square = 1 inch

turn the design over and retrace the design lines with the pencil.
Flip it back to the right side, and put the paper over the linen. Lightly
trace over the lines with a sharp pencil, thereby transferring the pencil
lines to the back of the linen. (These pencil marks will be easily
covered by the embroidery. Many embroidery books list other
methods of transfer, but mechanical transfer methods often stain the
cloth permanently.)

2. Following the stitch guide, using the project photograph on page

ALL LEAVES
ARE SATIN
LEAF STITCH

SATIN
STITCH

SATIN

SATIN

SATIN

SATIN

FRENCH
KNOT STITCH

CROSS
STITCH

SATIN
STITCH

FRENCH
KNOT

SATIN
STITCH

STITCH
GUIDE

SATIN
STITCH

SATIN
STITCH

SATIN
STITCH

SATIN
STITCH

LONG AND
SHORT STITCH

SATIN
STITCH

SATIN
STITCH

SATIN STITCH

LONG AND
SHORT
STITCH

ALL AREAS ARE DONE WITH
OUTLINE STITCH UNLESS
NOTED OTHERWISE

167

155 as a color guide, embroider all the flat areas of the picture. Work with the full six strands on all areas except for small details.

3. After all the flat areas are done, embroider the raised areas. Be careful when moving the hoop on the linen, for the raised areas can be marred easily.

4. Make and add the three-dimensional materials, following the project photograph for the proper placement. Make a 1½-inch-long braid ending in a ¾-inch-long tassel with the brown embroidery thread. Wrap the area between the braid and tassel with light blue thread. Attach the braid to the back of the head of the girl on the left, and tack it down under the blue wrapping. The feathers of the Indians should be bound and sewn in place next. Sew on the heads of wheat at the bottom of the picture. Sew the wheat stalks in lengths varying from 6¼ to 9¾ inches to the center of the picture to form the table top. To make the corn, make a long braid of yellow embroidery thread, fold it several times to create bulk, and wrap a piece of gauze around it to soften the color. Place it on the table and sew in place. Cut out ovals of sandpaper to suggest the earthenware plates and glue them in place with the matte medium. Make bowl shapes of sandpaper and glue them to the center of the table. Glue grain and beans inside. Put a heavy weight on each object as it is glued in place so that it will be pressed flat. Glue a pile of cardamom seeds in their husks to the lower right-hand side of the table.

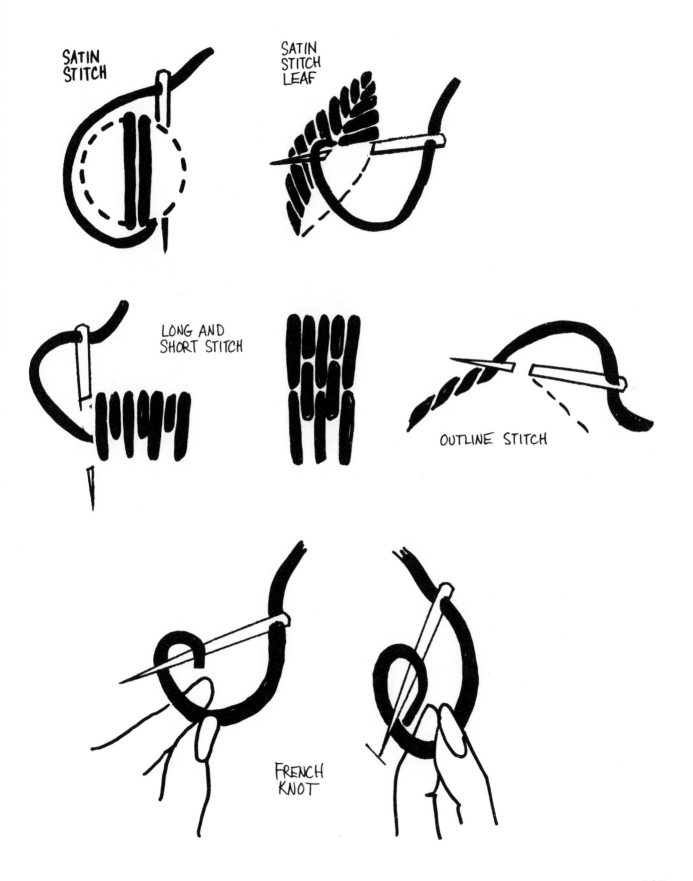

SATIN STITCH

SATIN STITCH LEAF

LONG AND SHORT STITCH

OUTLINE STITCH

FRENCH KNOT

CORNUCOPIA WITH CREAM PUFFS

Tools and Materials

12 frozen patty shells (2 packages) or homemade puff pastry
aluminum foil
ruler
scissors
paper clips
1 egg
pastry board
rolling pin
flour
pastry wheel or paring knife
pastry brush
2 baking sheets, greased and floured
granulated sugar
Cream Puffs (recipe follows)
pastry bag with ½-inch plain tip and a #30 star tip
1 cup heavy cream
¼ cup sugar

Instructions

1. Thaw the frozen patty shells at room temperature for 30 to 40 minutes or prepare your own from scratch.

2. Cut four 18-inch squares of aluminum foil with the scissors. Place one square on top of a second one and fold them in half diagonally to form a triangle. Repeat with the other two squares. Form each of the two triangles into cones, slightly overlapping the long edges, and place one inside the other so that the top edges are even. Turn ½ inch of the top edge of the cone toward the inside, crimping it a bit as you press it into place. Hold it in place at the top with paper clips.
3. Preheat oven to 425 degrees F.
4. Using a fork, beat egg slightly in a small bowl.
5. On a lightly floured board, place the patty shells in three rows of four each, overlapping each shell by ¾ inch. Using a lightly floured rolling pin, roll the shells into a long rectangle, stretching it so that it measures approximately 14 by 33 inches when you are finished. With a pastry wheel or sharp knife, cut the rolled pastry into twenty-two strips that are 1½ by 14 inches long each.
6. Beginning at the point of the cone and working toward the large opening, wind the strips of pastry around the shape. Each time you are about to add a strip, brush some of the beaten egg along the top ¼ inch of the edge of the strip below; then lap the new strip over the old by that amount. This will hold the pastry in place. Continue adding strips in this way until you have covered the entire foil shape.
7. Place the pastry-covered cornucopia on one of the baking sheets and sprinkle it lightly with sugar. Bake in the lower third of the oven for 10 to 15 minutes and then reduce the temperature to 375 degrees F. Continue baking for 10 to 15 minutes more—the *total* baking time should be about 25 minutes. Watch carefully to prevent the sugar from burning before the pastry is done.
8. Remove the cornucopia from the oven and cool it on a rack. When cool, carefully loosen the foil and remove it.
9. Prepare the cream puffs:

CREAM PUFFS
½ cup (1 stick) butter
¼ teaspoon salt
1 teaspoon sugar
1 cup flour
4 large eggs

Preheat oven to 425 degrees F. Place 1 cup warm water in a medium-size saucepan along with the butter, salt, and sugar. Bring to a boil, stirring occasionally with a wooden spoon. Remove from heat and add the flour all at once. Add the eggs one at a time, beating vigorously after each addition. Continue beating mixture vigorously with a wooden spoon until the dough forms a ball. Lightly grease and flour a baking sheet. Place the plain tip on the bottom of the pastry bag and fill the bag with the dough. Working on the baking sheet, squeeze out balls about the size of walnuts, leaving about 1½ inches of space between them. Bake for about 25 minutes or until puffy, crisp, and golden. Remove from oven, and place on rack to cool.
10. Fit the #30 star tip on the bottom of the pastry bag.

11. Whip the cream until it is almost stiff. Gradually add the ¼ cup sugar and continue beating until it is thick.

12. Fill the pastry bag with the whipped cream. Pierce a small hole on the top of each cream puff, using the point of a knife, Squeeze the whipped cream into each puff, and then, with a final spurt of whipped cream, create a star on top as you lift the pastry bag up.

13. Lay the cornucopia on a serving platter, and arrange the filled cream puffs inside and around in front of the cornucopia.

15

Hanukkah

Hanukkah—The Feast of Lights—is an eight-day moveable feast, taking place during the period from November to December. Celebrating the right to worship won by Judus Maccabeus and his forces over the decrees of King Antiochus of Syria, it begins with the lighting of the first candle of the menorah. Each day a new candle is lighted, carrying on the tradition started when the Maccabeans rededicated the temple in Jerusalem with only enough oil for one day—miraculously, the oil burned for eight days.

This is a family holiday, and for children, the high excitement is in receiving a gift each day for eight days. All the designs for the Hanukkah gift paper will make each gift a double surprise, and the menorah will light each day's celebration of dances and songs and feasting.

BLOCK-PRINTED STAR OF DAVID WRAPPING PAPER

Tools and Materials

pencil
tracing or typewriter paper, 8½ × 11 inches
1 sheet carbon paper, 8½ × 11½ inches
linoleum block, 4¼ × 6 inches
#1 X-acto knife with #11 blades
linoleum-block-cutting tools (available at art-supply stores)
water-solvent block-printing ink, in colors of your choice (available at art-supply stores)
large plate or square of glass, 6 × 6 inches
brayer
paper for printing, each 24 × 36 inches, such as white rice paper, brown Kraft paper, and blue drawing paper

Instructions

Cutting the design:
1. Trace the star design, including the dotted lines.

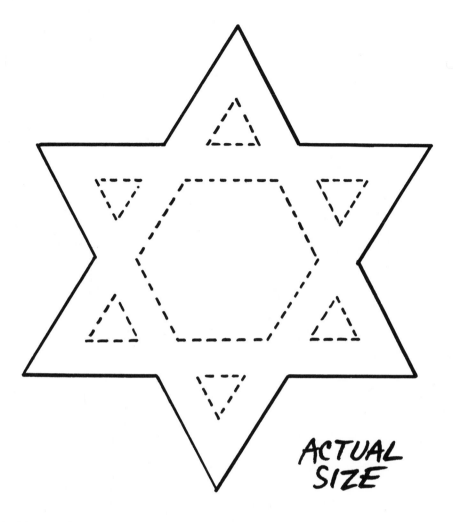

ACTUAL SIZE

2. Lay a piece of carbon paper, carbon side down, on the linoleum block, place the pattern on top, and trace around the design lines, transferring the pattern to the block.

3. Cut around the outer edge of the star shape with the X-acto knife. Using the linoleum-cutting tools, scoop out the background between the star and the edges of the block. Work from the star toward the edges so that you will not damage the sharp outline of the star. The solid star will form a raised pattern in the center of the block.

4. After printing several sheets of paper with the solid star on the linoleum block, wipe off all ink, leaving a clean surface. Using the carbon and pattern, transfer the dotted lines of the design to the linoleum. Recut the linoleum, following the dotted lines, removing the triangles and center section. The result will be a star design formed by ⅜-inch-wide intersecting lines.

Printing:

5. Squeeze water-solvent ink onto a large plate or square of glass. Add a few drops of water if necessary to thin it and mix well.

6. Roll the brayer over the ink, coating its surface with a thin film of color.

7. Roll the inked brayer over the surface pattern on the linoleum block. Turn the block over and apply it to the paper to be printed, pressing

175

down on the block with your fist to form an even-edged print. Repeat the process until the design is complete. Any slight irregularities in printing will only add to the beauty of the final effect. Let the printed paper dry flat for at least 24 hours.

Designs:

8. The easiest way to keep the rows of stars even as you print them is to match the points of one star with one already printed (the points will be visible at the edge of the block so that you will be able to see what you are doing.) Following are descriptions of how to make the designs shown in the photograph, but don't be limited by them. Create your own.

- Stars graduating from white to blue printed on brown Kraft paper: Print the first stars with white water-solvent block-printing ink and gradually add more blue ink as you print more until the final stars are dark blue.
- Stars arranged in a circular design printed in blue on white rice paper.
- Freeform star pattern printed on blue drawing paper: A row of five stars printed with almost-white ink, two rows with pinky-blue ink, and the rest with medium blue.
- White stars printed on blue drawing paper.

ARTGUM ERASER BLOCK-PRINTED STAR OF DAVID WRAPPING PAPER

To make this design, you will need artgum erasers and glue instead of a linoleum block. The rest of the procedure is almost the same—see the steps given below, which will refer you to the steps necessary in the linoleum-block printing instructions.

Tools and Materials

2 artgum erasers, standard rectangle size
epoxy or Krazy glue

Instructions

1. Glue the two artgum erasers together on the facing long sides, using epoxy or Krazy glue. Let dry for several hours.
2. Trace the pattern and transfer it to the eraser (see step 2).
3. Cut away the background and the center of the star, leaving the points raised above the background and center (see step 3).
4. Following the directions given in steps 5 through 7, print the design on rice paper with an allover pattern of blue stars.

ACTUAL SIZE

A CONTEMPORARY WOODEN MENORAH

Tools and Materials

hard pencil
ruler
1 sheet tracing paper, 18 × 24 inches
masking tape
1 piece plywood, ½ inch thick × 18 inches wide × 24 inches long
1 sheet carbon paper, 8½ × 11½ inches
jigsaw or coping saw
medium sandpaper
white glue
brace and bit or electric drill
varnish or shellac
paintbrush (for varnish or shellac)
9 screw-in metal candleholders (available at craft stores)

Instructions

1. With pencil and ruler on the tracing paper, enlarge the two parts of the menorah pattern by the grid method.

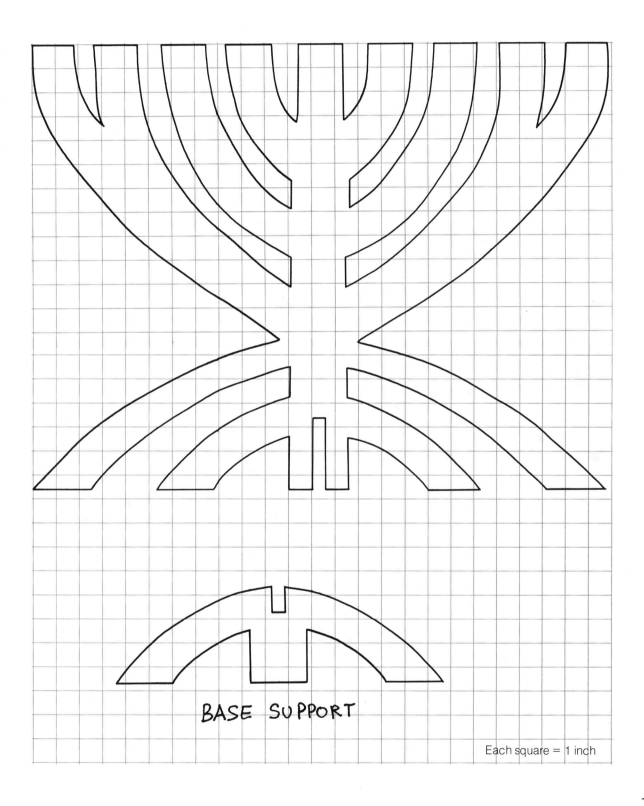

BASE SUPPORT

Each square = 1 inch

2. Tape the pattern to the plywood. Slide the sheet of carbon paper, carbon side down, between the tracing paper and the wood, moving the carbon along as you trace the pattern with a sharp, hard pencil.

3. With a jigsaw or coping saw, carefully cut out the menorah and the base support. Lightly sand the cut edges.

4. To attach the upper section to the curved base support, coat the matching areas with white glue. Insert the upper section into the lower section. Let dry.

6. Drill a starter hole for each of the nine candleholders in the center of each end of the nine wooden arms.

7. Apply a coat of varnish or shellac with a brush to all surfaces of the wood. When dry, screw in the candleholders and fill with candles.

16

Christmas

There is no one particular way to celebrate Christmas; each country has its own set of customs, developed over the centuries—and even each family has special ways of observing this holiday season. Occurring just after the shortest day of the year, Christmas is related to the old Roman festival of Saturnalia, during which green branches were carried through the streets and gifts of money were distributed. More recently, the brightly decorated Christmas tree has come to us from Germany, and St. Nicholas, the distributor of gifts in Holland, is the forerunner of our Santa Claus. One custom not so well known in the United States is Sweden's tradition of decorating a pole for the birds with straw and grain, a tradition that has given way to the "naturally decorated" Christmas tree adorned with straw and thin strips of wood.

In this section, you'll find projects based on many of these symbols of Christmas, beginning with birds' nests made of twine, twigs, and grass, to be hung on the tree and filled with bright decorations, candies, or nuts. A red Christmas poinsettia plant nestles on the shelf of the sturdy, wooden reindeer table, while around the base of the tree, a nostalgic train of decorated boxes holds gifts for family and friends. The wildly extravagant tree of shrimps and olives can be served before dinner or at a late afternoon gathering. And, for admiring or nibbling on all through the holidays, there are ginger angel cookies softly dusted with white sugar "snow."

BIRD'S-NEST TREE ORNAMENTS

Tools and Materials

5 Styrofoam balls, each 4 inches in diameter
aluminum foil
scissors
5 nails, each 4 to 5 inches long
hammer
5 blocks of wood, each about 1 inch thick × 6 inches wide × 6 inches
  long (you may also use heavy illustration board)
flour
white glue
food coloring in red, yellow, and green
large ball of twine
straight pins
small, flexible twigs
raffia
small watercolor brush

Instructions

1. Make molds for the nests by covering each Styrofoam ball with aluminum foil.

2. Drive a nail through the center of each wood block, working from bottom to top. Push a Styrofoam ball down over the point of each nail to a depth of 1 inch.

3. In a shallow bowl, mix flour with some water and add a little white glue to make a paste the consistency of pudding. Also mix food coloring in a small container in the proportion of four drops red to four drops yellow to one drop green. Stir enough of the color into the paste to turn it brown.

4. Saturate long lengths of twine in the paste and wind them around the upper half of each Styrofoam ball. Make the windings uneven and crisscrossed so that a mesh is created through which you can later weave raffia and twigs. Be sure to leave open spaces but pull the twine tight enough to retain the shape. Hold strands in place by thrusting pins through the twine into the Styrofoam.

5. After the twine is dry, remove pins and slip "nest" from each ball. You should have five stiff twine forms approximately 4¼ inches in diameter and 2¼ inches deep.

6. Begin weaving twigs and raffia in and out of the twine openings of each nest. To make the final result a full, natural-looking nest, also bring raffia and twigs over the top of each nest so that the top edges are rounded.

7. Paint the raffia with the food-coloring mixture and watercolor brush so that it is unevenly shaded.

8. Set the nests on the branches of a Christmas tree and then fill them with small Christmas balls, nuts in their shells, or wrapped hard candy. If desired, perch a small white china or feather bird on the edge of some of the nests.

WOODEN REINDEER TABLE

Tools and Materials

tracing paper, 8½ × 11 inches
masking tape
ruler
hard pencil
carbon paper, 8½ × 11½ inches
2 pieces plywood, each ½ inch thick × 36 inches wide × 42 inches long
jigsaw
medium sandpaper
1 piece plywood, ½ inch thick × 8 inches wide × 18 inches long (for shelf)
white glue
artist's paintbrush
1 can (8 ounces) oil-base wood stain, in oak
flat paintbrush (for wood stain)
grease crayon, in black
4 "L" brackets with screws, 2-inch size

Instructions

1. To make the two reindeer patterns, tape together enough tracing paper to make two sheets, each 36 by 42 inches. Using the grid method, enlarge one pattern on one sheet of paper by following only the solid lines. Make a second pattern by substituting the dotted lines

Each square = 1 inch

on the two legs and ear for the solid.

2. Tape enough carbon paper together to make one sheet 36 by 42 inches.

3. Lay the sheet of carbon, carbon side down, over the better side of one 36- by 42-inch piece of wood; lay one of the enlarged patterns on top. Transfer the design to the wood by tracing around the outline and

the design line with a hard pencil. Place the carbon paper on the second large piece of wood; lay the second pattern, *pencil side down*, over the carbon paper, and trace over the lines that show through the tracing paper pattern. Be sure to trace the second pattern pencil side down; otherwise the two reindeer pieces will face in opposite directions.

4. Cut out the two reindeer shapes with the jigsaw.

5. Lightly sand all wood surfaces, including the 8- by 18-inch shelf piece.

6. On the outside of both reindeer pieces, paint white glue on all areas—the body spots, the belly, the outer edge of the tail, the center of the ear, and the eyes—that should remain softly offwhite when the pieces are stained. Let glue dry thoroughly.

7. Stain all three pieces on both sides with oak stain, using the flat brush and following the manufacturer's directions. Be sure to allow the stain to dry before turning the pieces over.

8. Draw in the nose and eyes on the outside of both reindeer pieces with the black grease crayon.

9. Following the diagram, attach "L" brackets to the bottom of the shelf on opposite edges of the 18-inch side. Attach the other half of

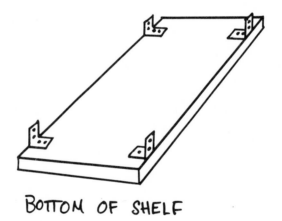

BOTTOM OF SHELF

each bracket to the corresponding position on the inside of each reindeer piece.

SHELF WITH
BRACKETS UNDERNEATH

10. If desired, set a poinsettia plant on the shelf.

A CHRISTMAS-BOX TRAIN

Although there is considerable flexibility in the size of the boxes you choose to use for your train, we've specified approximate sizes for them because they must be in proportion to each other. When you've completed your train, fill the boxes with gifts and stand the cars, train-style, around the Christmas tree.

Tools and Materials

throwaway, cone-shaped, plastic cup, 8-ounce size, such as a Solo cup
ruler
scissors
posterboard, in a variety of colors
rubber cement
cylindrical cardboard container, about 3 inches in diameter and 10 inches long, such as a bread-crumb container
#1 X-acto knife with #11 blades
wooden sewing-thread spool
acrylic paints, in a variety of bright colors
2 round watercolor brushes: #2 and #8
at least 9 colored cardboard gift boxes with lids: 1 box (for bottom of engine cab) approximately 12 inches long × 5 inches wide × 5 inches deep; 1 box (for middle of cab) approximately 5 inches wide × 5 inches long × 3 inches deep; 1 jewelry-size box (for top of cab); 3 boxes (for cars), each approximately 12 inches long × 10 inches wide × 9 inches deep, 1 box (for bottom of caboose) approximately 6 inches long × 6 inches wide × 6 inches deep; and 1 jewelry-size box (for top of caboose)
transparent tape
flint paper, in a variety of bright colors
typewriter paper, 8½ × 11 inches
cardboard tube from roll of paper towels
corrugated cardboard (for wheels)
brass paper fasteners
glitter
1 can spray enamel, in red (optional)
stick-on stars, in gold

187

Instructions

1. Start by making the smokestack for the engine, which is in two sections. The lower, angled piece is made with the plastic cup. To make the upper part, cut a 3- by 11-inch piece of posterboard. Cut eight evenly spaced, ½-inch-deep pie-shaped wedges into one 11-inch edge. Form into a cylinder, overlapping the matching 3-inch-long edges about ¼ inch, and cement together. Coat ¾ inch of the upper inside edge of the cup with rubber cement, and set the cylinder, wedge-cut end down, into the cup. Let the cement dry.

2. Use the cardboard cylinder to make the boiler. With the X-acto knife, cut a hole in one side of the box toward one end, making it slightly larger than the bottom of the cup. (This end will become the top and front of the boiler.) Push the cup into the hole. Glue a wooden spool at the other end of the top of the boiler. Paint the boiler, smokestack, and wooden spool in a color to match or contrast with the color of the box for the engine.

3. To make the cab, cement a jewelry box in the center of the top (lid) of the square box for the middle of the cab. Cut two C-shaped pieces from the posterboard, following the diagram for shape, to the height

of the square box. With transparent tape, attach each C piece to one side of the square box ¼ inch in from each corner, as shown in the diagram. Then cut two slots in the corresponding edge of the lid of the

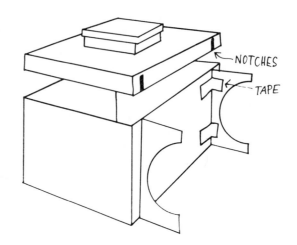

box, each ¼ inch in from the corner. Set the lid on the box so that the slots fit over the tops of the two C pieces, holding them in place. Spread cement over the bottom of the square box and C pieces and cement them to the top of the box designated for the bottom of the cab, positioning it toward one end. Cut a piece of flint paper 1 inch longer than the distance between the C-shaped pieces and ½ inch wider. Fold down ½ inch on the two short sides and one long side. Sawtooth the three folded-down edges and cement the pieces over the C pieces to make a valanced canopy, as shown in the diagram.

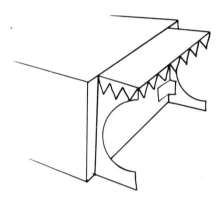

4. Enlarge the cowcatcher and engine support patterns by the grid method on typewriter paper and cut them both out with scissors. Lay

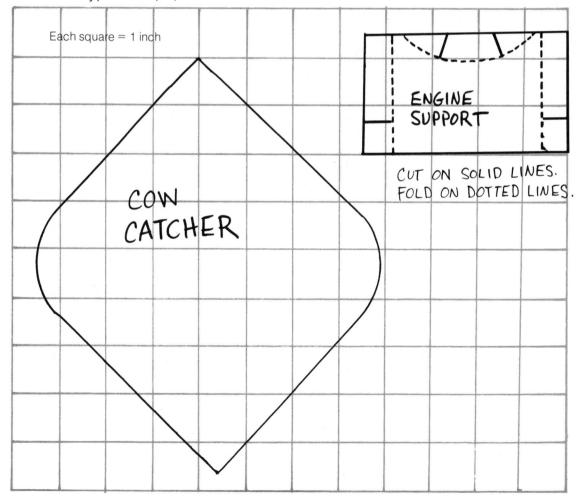

Each square = 1 inch

COW CATCHER

ENGINE SUPPORT

CUT ON SOLID LINES.
FOLD ON DOTTED LINES.

them on a piece of posterboard, trace around them, and cut out one of each. Curve the cowcatcher into shape and cement it to the

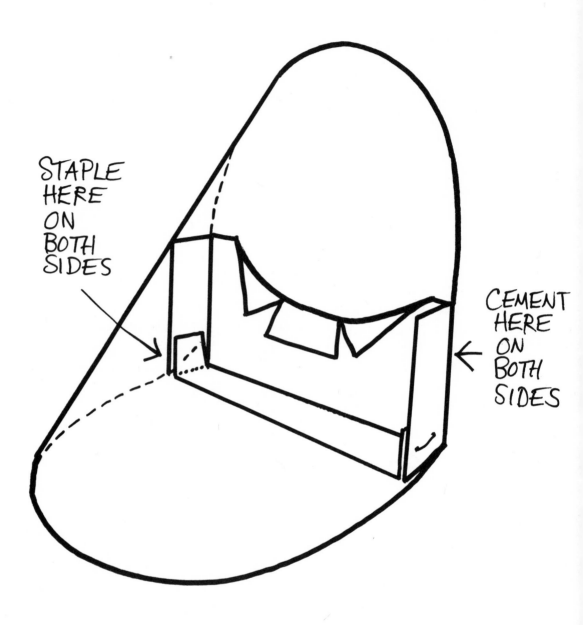

STAPLE
HERE
ON
BOTH
SIDES

CEMENT
HERE
ON
BOTH
SIDES

support, as shown. Cement the support to the front of the boiler, as shown.

5. The final step for the boiler is to make the wheels and wheel supports. To make the supports, cut the cardboard tube in half. Then cut out a small center section on one side of each half for the curved part of the boiler to set into (see diagram). Cement them in place on

the boiler and paint them with acrylic paint. Cut four disks, each about 2 inches in diameter, from the corrugated cardboard for the wheels and paint them with acrylic paint in the same color as the supports. Push a paper fastener through the center of each wheel. Cement the wheels to the ends of the supports.

6. Cut four wheels from the corrugated cardboard for the engine cab area, each about 4 inches in diameter. Paint them a bright color and add them to the sides of the engine cab by pushing a paper fastener through the center of each wheel and into the box, fanning the wings of the fastener on the inside of the box to hold the wheels securely. To decorate the wheels with spokes, fold a circle of contrasting flint paper that is slightly smaller than the diameter of the wheels over four times to make a triangle; then make a triangular cut into the open edge, as shown in the diagram. Unfold the triangle and cement it to a wheel. Repeat for the other three wheels.

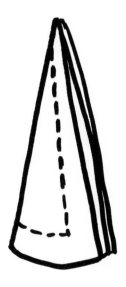

7. To decorate the first car of the train, enlarge the window design by the grid method. Cut it out. Trace two copies on flint paper in a color that will contrast with that of the car and carefully cut them out with the X-acto knife. Cement one on each side of one of the large boxes. To make the scalloped edge on top of the car, cut out four

Each square = 1 inch

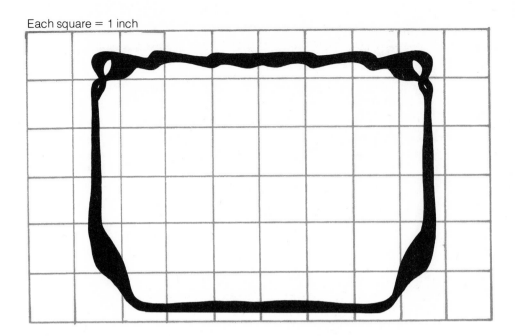

1½-inch-wide strips of posterboard to the dimensions of the top of the box. Scallop the edges and cement them to the sides of the lid, with scallops facing up.

8. To decorate the circus-wagon car, cut twenty-six ¼-inch-wide strips, each about 5½ inches long, from a contrasting color of flint paper. Cement thirteen on each side of another of the large boxes, as shown in the diagram. Trim the bottoms of each end strip by about ½

inch so that they will end above the wheels. Paint a line of cement around the bars to make a frame and cover it with glitter. Add a scalloped edge to the top as described in step 7.

9. Make the caboose next with the box for the caboose and a jewelry box. Spray both with red paint if you wish. Cement the small box to the center of the top of the larger box. Cut four 2-inch-diameter disks from the corrugated cardboard for wheels, paint them in a contrasting color, and attach them with paper fasteners, as described in step 6.

10. Add a third large box to the other two regular cars of the train. Then finish decorating the train by adding windows. Cut rectangles of flint paper in various colors to fit the sides of the cab, the third box just added, and the caboose (see the project photograph if you wish more specific guidance). If you wish to suggest window shades, as we did on the third car, cut shorter rectangles in different colors and cement them over the window rectangles. Finally, add a few gold stars to the third box, placing them at random.

11. Cut twelve 3-inch-diameter disks from the corrugated cardboard to make wheels for the three large cars. Attach them with paper fasteners and decorate them with spokes as described in step 6.

SHRIMP CHRISTMAS TREE

Although this red-and-green shrimp centerpiece is expensive to make, it adds such a festive note to a Christmas open house or cocktail party that it's worth the splurge. After all, Christmas comes but once a year. Of course, if you wish, you can start with a smaller Styrofoam cone and decorate it with smaller shrimp.

Tools and Materials

Styrofoam cone, 15 to 18 inches high with a base diameter of 8 inches
   (you can also carve one from a large block of Styrofoam)
plastic wrap
5 pounds jumbo shrimp
5 pounds large shrimp
large saucepan
½ cup fresh lemon juice
slotted spoon
colander
about 40 green olives stuffed with pimientos
large plate
toothpicks
large serving dish

Instructions

1. Wrap the Styrofoam cone with clear plastic wrap so that shrimps will not come in contact with it.

2. Clean the shrimps by removing the outer shell; you can either leave the tails on or remove them. If any of the shrimps have a dark vein, carefully remove it with a pointed knife or toothpick.

3. In a large, covered saucepan, bring 3 cups of water to a rolling boil; add the ½ cup of lemon juice.

4. Drop ten to fifteen shrimp into the boiling liquid; cover and cook 2 to 3 minutes. Remove shrimps from the liquid with the slotted spoon and drain in the colander.

5. Add another ten to fifteen shrimps to the hot liquid in the pan. When the water returns to a boil, cook shrimps only 2 to 3 minutes and then remove with the slotted spoon. Repeat procedure until all shrimps are cooked.

6. While shrimps are cooking, slice each olive in half crosswise and set aside.

7. Set the Styrofoam shape on a large plate. Using toothpicks, attach a row of jumbo shrimp all around the bottom of the cone: Turn each shrimp so that its curved back faces outward and its wide end is up, push the blunt end of a toothpick through the wide end, and then thrust the pointed end of the toothpick into the Styrofoam. Fit the tops of the shrimps fairly closely together as you add more shrimp to the row. When that row is completed, add another row of jumbo shrimp just above, placing each shrimp so that its tail is between two thick tops of the shrimp on the row below. Continue to add rows of shrimp in this way, using shrimps that are progressively smaller as you work toward the top of the cone, until the cone is covered.

8. Decorate each row with the olive halves, thrusting the blunt end of a toothpick into the Styrofoam between each shrimp and then placing an olive half on the tip of each toothpick so that the cut portion of the olive is facing outward. Continue with this procedure until you reach the top of the tree. Then arrange five or six shrimps around the tip of the cone to form a cylinder. Using another toothpick, attach a final shrimp through the center of the cylinder so that its tail extends outward.

9. Carefully place the centerpiece in a festive serving dish—have someone help you if it is too heavy for you to lift alone—and surround it with chipped ice. Place a bowl of seafood sauce or cocktail sauce beside the shrimp to use as a dip.

SUGAR-SIFTED ANGEL COOKIES

The ginger cookie dough for this project must be refrigerated overnight before it can be worked with, so plan ahead. Makes approximately 18 cookies.

Tools and Materials

ruler
felt-tipped marking pen, in black
tracing paper, 8½ × 11 inches
white glue
1 sheet heavy, uncorrugated cardboard, about 8½ × 11 inches
scissors
1 sheet stencil paper, 9 × 12 inches
masking tape
#1 X-acto knife with #11 blades
manila file folder
Gingerbread Cookie Dough (recipe follows)
baking sheet
wire sifter
confectioners sugar
small artist's paintbrush

Instructions

1. Using the marking pen and the tracing paper, trace the angel design. Glue the design to one side of the piece of cardboard and

ACTUAL
SIZE

197

allow it to dry.

2. Trim the stencil paper to measure 7½ by 10 inches and tape it in place over the design.

3. Holding the X-acto knife exactly as you would a pencil, begin cutting out the designs showing through the stencil paper. Always cut toward yourself, allowing the knife to glide along over the lines; do not cut too deeply into the cardboard beneath the stencil paper. Cut away all interior shapes and then cut the stencil out along the outside black line.

4. Next, trace around the cookie-cutout line (the outside black line) on an opened manila file folder. Cut out the design with scissors; this will be your cookie pattern.

5. Prepare the Gingerbread Cookie Dough:

1 cup (2 sticks) butter or margarine, at room temperature
¼ cup shortening, at room temperature
1½ cups sugar
2 eggs
⅔ cup molasses
6 cups all-purpose flour
1 teaspoon baking soda
1 teaspoon salt
4 teaspoons cinnamon
2 teaspoons powdered ginger

In a large mixing bowl, combine butter, shortening, and sugar; beat with a spoon till light and fluffy. Beat in eggs and molasses until blended. In another bowl, mix half the flour with the baking soda, salt, cinnamon, and ginger. Combine these dry ingredients with the other ingredients in the bowl. Now stir in as much of the remaining flour as is needed to make a stiff dough. Divide the dough in half, wrap in plastic food wrap, and refrigerate overnight.

6. Preheat oven to 325 degrees F. Remove half the dough from the refrigerator. Roll out on a lightly floured surface to a ⅛-inch thickness. Because this dough has a high butter content, you must work fairly quickly or it will soften. Using a sharp knife to draw around the pattern you have made, cut out as many cookies as will fit on your baking sheet. Transfer each cookie with a spatula to an ungreased baking sheet, leaving ½-inch spaces between each cookie. Bake for about 15 minutes or until the cookies are firm and golden. Remove from the pan with the spatula, and cool on racks. Refrigerate all cookie scraps immediately so that the dough will have a chance to stiffen before you reuse it. Repeat process with second roll of dough and scraps until all angel cookies are baked. *Makes approximately 18 cookies.*

7. Place a single angel cookie on a plate and center the stencil over the top. Holding the small wire sifter in one hand and a small amount of confectioners sugar in the other, begin moving the sifter back and forth as you sprinkle sugar into it. Only a light sprinkling is necessary. When the exposed areas are coated with sugar, gently lift the stencil away from the cookie *straight up.* Remove cookie carefully to a flat serving platter. Continue stenciling the remaining cookies in the same

way until all have been decorated. If any of your stenciled designs appear to be messy, simply dip the tip of the small brush into water and gently "paint away" any mistakes.

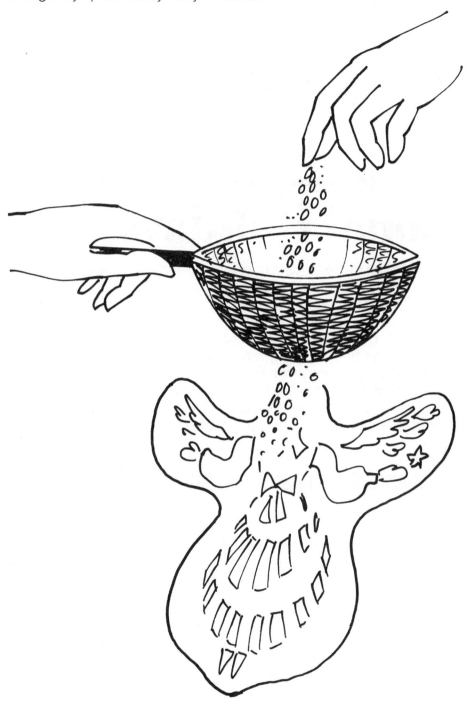

17

Personal Holidays

There is never a reason not to celebrate a day, for someone you know is surely having a birthday, getting engaged or married, having a shower, graduating, celebrating Mother's or Father's Day, moving to a new home, going off on an extended trip, just completing a major project, retiring, or starting a new job—the occasions worthy of gifts are countless. Presents are bought and given but a unique, one-of-a-kind special gift, card, or gift wrapping can make that gift a very personal one. Here are many ideas for gifts and gift wrappings that are simple to make and beautiful to receive. You will find that the matching cards, which are suitable for framing, may become treasured mementos of the occasion.

A CHAMP'S LOUNGING ROBE

Tools and Materials

man's lounging robe pattern (we used McCall's pattern #5368)
6 yards satin: 4 yards in red and 2 yards in yellow
2 sheets typewriter paper, each 8½ × 11 inches
ruler
pencil
scissors
2 yards Stitch-witchery
straight pins
iron
thread, in red and yellow
sewing machine (zigzag attachment optional)
needle (optional)

Instructions

1. Follow pattern instructions for cutting out the robe. Cut the collar, belt, cuffs, and pockets from yellow satin; cut the main pieces from the red. If the pattern does not include cuffs, cut two 8-inch-wide pieces of yellow satin, each long enough to go around the bottom of the sleeves plus ½ inch extra for a side seam. On each length, sew the 8-inch sides together with a ¼-inch seam, right sides facing each other. Slip one of the circles of yellow satin over the end of one sleeve, right sides together. Sew the bottom of the cuff to the bottom of the sleeve with a ¼-inch seam. Bring the top, raw edge down and over the bottom seam, turn under the raw edge, and fasten it with hemming stitches on the inside of the sleeve. Tack the upper folded edge to the sleeve if necessary. Repeat the procedure with the other cuff and sleeve.

2. Enlarge the letters in "CHAMP" by the grid method and cut them

Each square = 1 inch

out. Draw the symbol "#" to 2⅜ inches square, and make the number "1" 4½ inches high.

3. Cut out the letters, the "#," and the "1" from both the yellow satin and the Stitch-witchery. Space out the letters across the back section of the robe, working from armhole to armhole but staying outside the armhole seam area. The distance from the center of the neck seam to the top of the center "A" should be 6½ inches. Curve the line of letters so that the bottoms of the two end letters are 1⅞ inches lower than the bottom of the "A." The length of the entire word should be about 19 inches. Sandwich the Stitch-witchery letters between the satin letters and robe and iron in place, following the manufacturer's directions. Stitch with yellow thread around the edges of the letters, using a zigzag attachment on a sewing machine. This stitching not only forms a decoration but covers the raw edges of the letters. (If you do not have a zigzag attachment, cut letters ⅛ to ¼ inch larger all around, turn this amount of extra material under as a hem, and baste in place. Then iron the letters in position with Stitch-witchery. Stitch around the letters with a plain sewing-machine stitch, 1/16 inch in from the edges.)

4. Place the "#" and the "1" on the left front side of the robe, centering them on the width. Place the Stitch-witchery pieces between the "#" and the "1" and the fabric and iron in place.

5. Stitch all the pieces of the robe together, following pattern instructions.

PRESSED-FLOWER CARD AND GIFT WRAP

For this project, we have specified acrylic medium in a matte finish; however you may prefer to use the glossy finish. If so, you will have to cover the entire card with it or the gloss will appear uneven. The acrylic medium seals and protects the dried arrangements. If you wish to store several cards or pieces of wrapping paper, place sheets of wax paper between them for protection.

Tools and Materials

weeds, flowers, leaves, and grass collected from the countryside
paper towels
thread, in tan
stiff paper, such as BFK Rives, Arches, rough rice papers, or other printing papers (for the card)
ruler
scissors
small jar acrylic matte medium, such as Liquitex
soft, artist's paintbrush, ½ inch wide
thin paper, such as tissue paper, rice paper, or charcoal paper (for the box)
satin ribbon, ¼ inch wide, any color
gift box

Instructions

1. Combine flowers, weeds, leaves, and grasses on paper towels into as many arrangements as you'd like for the card and wrapping paper. Tie a small piece of sewing thread around the stems of each group to hold them together. Cover with more paper toweling. Carefully place the toweling holding the designs between the pages of a heavy book and leave them there for three or four days to dry completely.

2. When the plant materials have dried, remove them from the book. Then measure the paper for the card, making it large enough so that there will be plenty of space around the design. Double one of the measurements to form the back of the card. Then cut out the card.

3. Fold the card in half and place the arrangement on the front.

4. Mix a small amount of the acrylic matte medium with water, using half medium with half water. Carefully brush this liquid over the flowers and leaves. The thin areas will be the first to absorb it. If this mixture is not strong enough to hold the stems and thick flowers in place, use full-strength acrylic matte medium. Let the design dry for several hours.

5. Tie a bow of the ribbon and use full-strength acrylic matte medium to attach it to the cluster of grass and flower stems. Frame the arrangement with more ribbon by brushing a thin line of acrylic matte medium on the paper and pressing the ribbon into position. To make the corners, either fold or cut the ribbon.

6. Wrap the gift box with the chosen thin paper. Use several strands of ribbon to tie the package and make a bow.

7. Place a dried arrangement on top of the package. Working on only one side at a time, carefully brush on the acrylic matte medium/water mixture to attach the design to the paper. Let dry.

8. Apply more dried materials in the same way to a side adjacent to the top.

COLLAGE GIFT BOX AND CARD

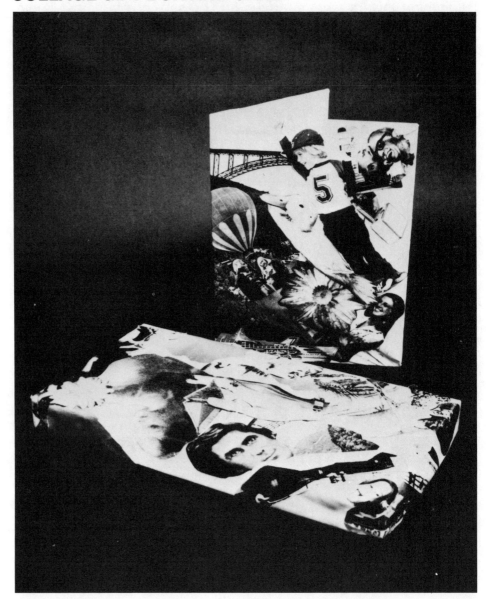

Decorating with collage is a very simple way to personalize a gift box and card; it is also inexpensive since it can be done with materials found around the house. Since there is no specific design pattern in this project, you can make your collaged box and card any size you wish.

Tools and Materials

magazines
scissors
stationery or candy box with lid
1 piece bristol board (for the card)
white glue
facial tissues
ribbon (optional)

Instructions

1. Flip through the color pages, including the advertisements, of several magazines and cut out elements from the pictures that will form a pleasing overall pattern on the box and card. The fun in doing this is in the sometimes-strange juxtaposing of objects: large with the small with no relation to reality or modern with the historical or antique, such as a pyramid set in the middle of a green forest. Any combination that will turn your decoration into a fantasy world will work. You can select pictures that are all within a given color range or theme but, in general, just be loose.
2. Arrange the cutout elements on the top and sides of the box lid, and on the front and back of the piece of bristol board folded over.
3. Glue down all the elements with white glue applied sparingly—you do not want it to soak through the thin magazine paper. Pat down each piece with several facial tissues crumpled into a soft ball, removing the excess glue that will leak out from under the edges of the pictures and gently smoothing out any air bubbles trapped under the pictures. Allow to dry.
4. Tie the box with ribbon if you wish, and write a message on the inside of the card.

ORIGAMI CARDS

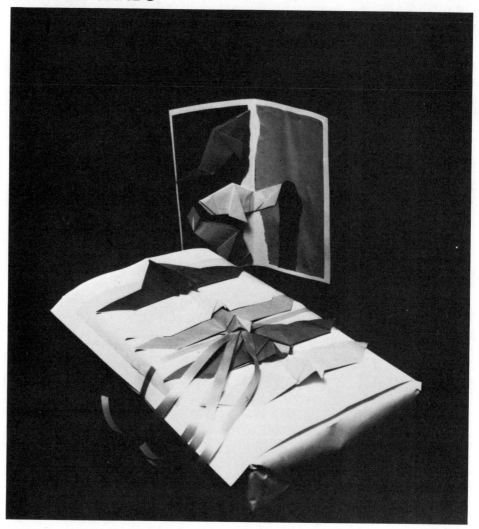

Tools and Materials

origami paper, in a variety of colors (available at art-supply stores)
ruler
soft pencil
scissors
2-ply bristol or other stiff paper, in white
white glue
gift box
gift-wrapping paper, solid color or subtly patterned
transparent tape
ribbon

Instructions

1. Several designs for decorating cards and boxes are shown and described in the following illustrations. For other design sources, look through an origami instruction book or follow one of the designs

included in some packets of origami paper. To get the feeling of working with the paper and to see the three-dimensional quality of the various designs, fold a number of designs before you begin the actual project. Then choose one of those designs to decorate the card and gift-wrapped box. Make sure that the origami papers you are using are true squares; if not, measure and trim them accordingly.

2. The Pigeon is a simple design to cut and fold. To decorate the gift box shown in the project photograph, fold five pigeons, each in a different color, following the diagrams below. Lay the pigeons one

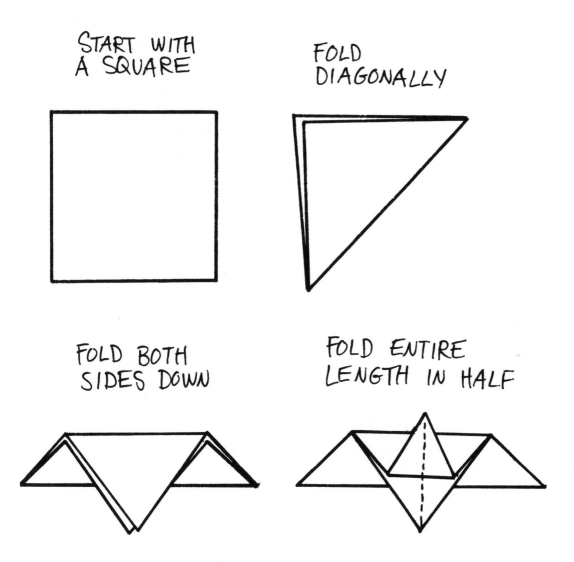

START WITH
A SQUARE

FOLD
DIAGONALLY

FOLD BOTH
SIDES DOWN

FOLD ENTIRE
LENGTH IN HALF

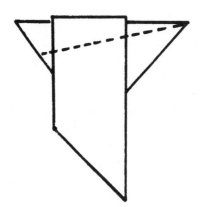

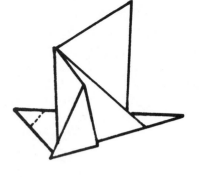

FOLD WINGS UP

AFTER WINGS
ARE UP
FOLD HEAD
DOWN

FOLD
HEAD
DOWN   AND

THEN
INVERT

above the other on a piece of bristol paper. Using a ruler and pencil, draw a rectangle around the group, allowing a few inches for a border all around. Cut out the rectangle. Set the birds aside and add a sky to the rectangle by covering two-thirds of it with a light blue origami paper; use white glue to apply it. Leave uncovered an inch or so of the bristol around the top and sides to make a white border. Replace the birds on the paper, centering them over the card and making sure that they line up one above the other inside the center fold. Next, lightly glue down only the parts of the pigeons that touch the surface of the bristol. As you glue each piece, weight it with a small book or two until it is dry; then fold the card in half lengthwise so that the birds are on the outside of the card. Wrap the gift box and lay the card on top of the box; tie a length of ribbon around it to hold it in place.

3. The Fish is a bit more complicated to fold, but by following the diagram, you will be able to make this fascinating design. To make

START WITH A
SQUARE

FOLD
DIAGONALLY

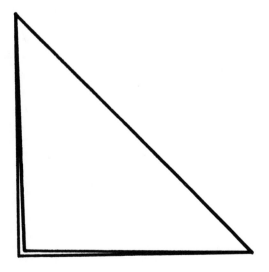

OPEN AND FOLD DIAGONALLY FROM OTHER SIDES

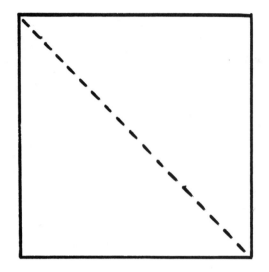 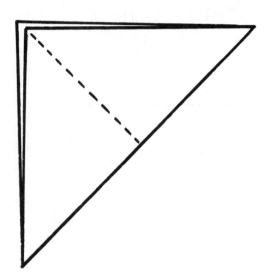

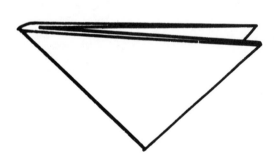

FOLD TOWARDS CENTER

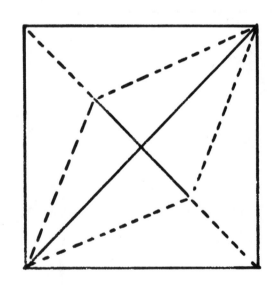

FOLD IN ALONG CREASES

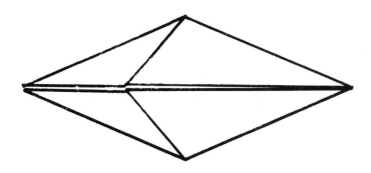

FOLD IN HALF
ALONG LENGTH

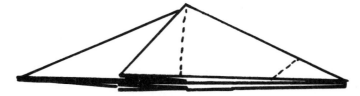

FOLD FINS BACK
AND TAIL UP

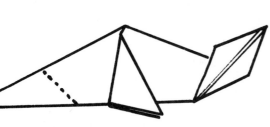

AND
OVER AND
TUCK EXTENDING
FLAP
INSIDE BODY

FOLD HEAD
UP

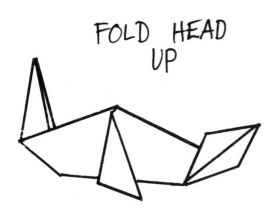

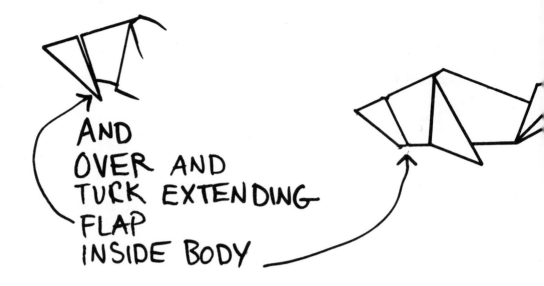

AND
OVER AND
TUCK EXTENDING
FLAP
INSIDE BODY

the card, fold three fish, one each in orange, yellow, and light green, for the inside of the card and one in gray for the outside. Arrange the first three fish on a piece of bristol paper. Add a few inches all around the fish and draw a rectangle that size. Then cut out the rectangle and fold it in half crosswise. Cut a piece of dark blue origami paper slightly smaller than half the card. Then tear one long edge of the paper unevenly. With the torn edge along the fold of the card, glue the paper to the top half of the inside of the card. Repeat this procedure with a piece of light gray origami paper and glue it to the bottom half of the inside of the card, placing the torn edge along the fold and leaving a bit of white space between the two torn edges. If you wish, add a torn green shape or two to the scene to suggest seaweed. Arrange the fish on the card and glue the pieces down only where they touch the paper. Weight them with a book or two until they are dry. Glue the gray fish to the front half of the card in the same way; tear a bit of green paper for seaweed and add it; and finish the scene with some gray circles to suggest air bubbles.

4. Carefully press the cards in a heavy book to flatten the bristol paper and the glued designs.

RHINESTONE AND BUGLE-BEAD SUNBURST GIFT BOX AND CARD

Tools and Materials

1 spray can glossy enamel, in royal blue
1 box with lid, at least 5 inches square (depth is unimportant)
1 piece illustration board, 4½ × 4½ inches
ruler
pencil
#1 X-acto knife with #11 blades
compass
multipurpose cement
typewriter paper, 8½ × 11 inches (optional)
160 yellow rhinestones, each ⅛ inch (full) in diameter
tweezers
64 red bugle beads, each ¼ inch long
192 silver bugle beads, each 3/16 inch long
48 orange bugle beads, each ¼ inch long

Instructions

1. Spray the box, lid, and piece of illustration board with the enamel; allow it to dry.

2. In the center of the box lid, lightly draw two circles with the compass: the outer one, 2¼ inches in diameter; the inner one, 1¾ inches in diameter. Starting at the edge of the inner circle, add eight 1-inch-long radiating lines around the circumference, following the diagram for the placement of lines. You may want to make this

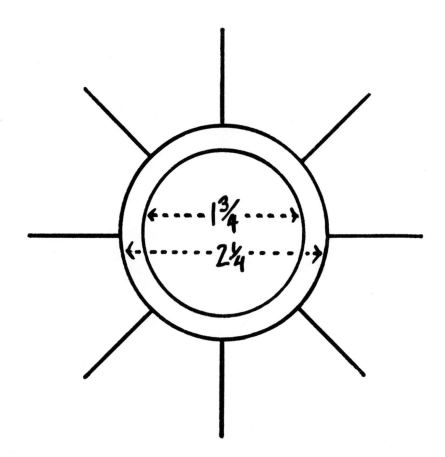

diagram on a sheet of typewriter paper first and place the bead pattern in position. Then transfer the beads to the box lid.

3. Spread the multipurpose cement over the surface of the inner circle on the box lid. Fill the 1¾-inch circle with rhinestones, starting at the outer edge and overlapping the pencil lines just a little so that they will be covered. Use the tweezers to help place the rhinestones in position. There should be approximately twenty-eight rhinestones around the outer edge; twenty-two in the next ring; sixteen in the next; then ten; and finally four in the center. These amounts may vary, depending on the size of the rhinestones.

4. Spread cement over the outer circle area and lay a line of four red bugle beads end to end over each of the eight radiating pencil lines. Work from the edge of the inner circle outward.

5. Between each red bugle-bead line, form a pyramid of silver bugle

beads: First lay three beads vertically on each side of the red line so that one end of each touches the inner circle line; form the row above by laying two beads vertically on each side; and make the final row by laying one bead on each side. The top red bead should stand alone, forming the top of the pyramid.

6. Fill in between each pyramid with three orange bugle beads, laying them horizontally one above the other so that the bottom bead lies on the inner-circle line and working outward.

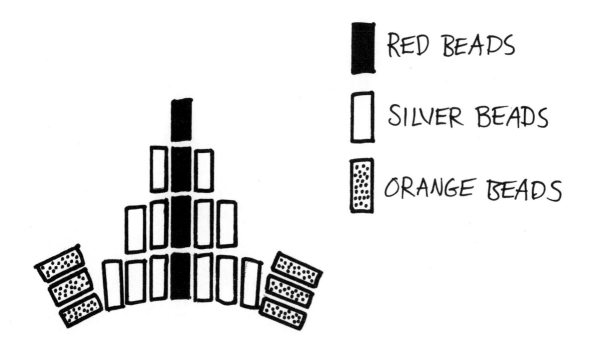

RED BEADS

SILVER BEADS

ORANGE BEADS

7. For the card, repeat the sunburst design in the center of the piece of painted illustration board, making the design the same size as the one on the box.

ALPHABET-SOUP MESSAGE GIFT BOX AND CARD

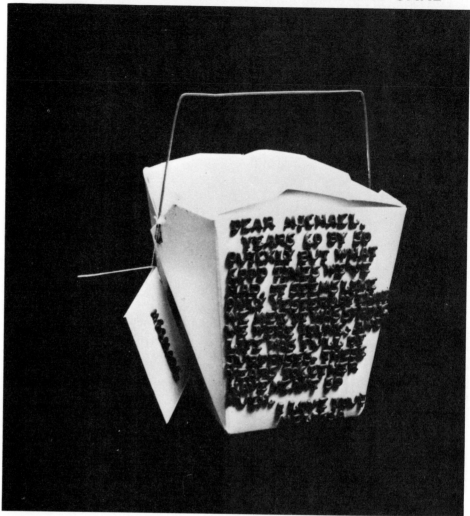

The base for this project is a Chinese food take-out carton, which you can get from most Chinese restaurants. To make sure that it is unused, offer to pay for it. The next step is to decide what you'd like to say in your message. Here is the message, broken down line by line, we used on our box.

Dear Michael
Years go by so
quickly but what
good times we've
had, it seems like
only yesterday that
we met. It was spring,
we were young, and
life was full of
surprises. These
years together
have meant so
much.
I love you!
    Melissa

Tools and Materials

#32 cardboard take-out container, 4⅜ inches high × 3¾ inches
   across the top × 2¾ inches across the bottom
typewriter paper, 8½ × 11 inches
pencil
alphabet soup-noodles
newspapers or cardboard
1 spray can paint, in green
fine-pointed watercolor brush
white glue
1 piece illustration board, 2⅜ × 3⅜ inches, in white

Instructions

1. Decide whether you'd like the message you've chosen to appear on just one side of the cardboard container, on two sides, or run around all four sides of it in a strip. If you want it to be on just one side, lay the container on its side and draw around it on a piece of typewriter paper. If you want it to be on two sides, draw around the container twice. If you want it to run around in a strip, outline all four sides.

2. Pick out the letters necessary to spell your message and lay them out within the outline(s) you have drawn. If your message will be longer than one line, slightly indent the first letter of the second line and any further lines so that the left-hand side will follow the angle of the container; allow the right-hand side to be staggered. This layout will serve as your guide later when you are gluing the letters to the actual container. Also pick out the letters necessary to spell the recipient's name, and lay them aside.

3. Spread out all the letters you'll be using, right side up, on folded newspaper or a sheet of cardboard and spray them with the green paint. Hold the can some distance away from the letters so that the pressure doesn't make them jump around. Allow them to dry.

4. Carefully remove the metal handle of the container and lay it on the newspaper or cardboard. Spray it with two or three coats of green paint, allowing drying time between each coat. When the paint is thoroughly dry and hard, replace the handle on the box. If any paint chips off, touch up the bare spots by dabbing them with a brush moistened with the spray paint.

5. When the letters are dry, paint the backs of those for the message with white glue and the watercolor brush. Lay the container on one of its sides and position the letters on the side now on top according to the plan you worked out in step 2. Once the glue has dried, be careful not to squeeze the container or the letters may pop off.

6. Fold the piece of illustration board in half the long way. Apply glue to the backs of the letters for the recipient's name and position them on the front half, centering the letters on the depth.

MARBLEIZED GIFT PAPER

Use this delicate, multicolored paper to wrap small gifts or to cover books and personal journals.

Tools and Materials

disposable aluminum roasting pan, 9 × 12 or 9 × 15 inches
newspaper
3 paper cups
3 tubes oil paints: one each in viridian green, alizarin crimson, and
   burnt sienna
measuring cup
turpentine
flat, wooden stirring sticks
typewriter paper, 8½ × 11 inches, or other paper no larger than
   roasting pan

Instructions

1. Half fill with water the roasting pan. Spread newspaper over a flat surface under and beside the pan.

2. To prepare the liquid color, add about a tablespoon of each different color to a paper cup. Measure out ¼ cup of turpentine for each color. Blend the liquid slowly into the color, mixing well with a wooden stick until each color is dissolved and free of lumps.

3. Add 1 tablespoon of each color mixture to the water in the pan, placing the color in separate areas. The liquid color will float on top of the water. Lightly stir the water with a circular motion a few times. Before the water has stopped moving, drop a sheet of paper flat on the surface of the water. Do not submerge or "dunk" the paper but allow it to float on the surface for just a moment. Then quickly lift the paper up and out. Turn it over rapidly and lay it, marbleized surface up, flat on the newspaper to dry for a day or two.

4. From the first mixture in the pan, several more sheets of paper can be marbleized in this way, although each will have less color on it than the one before. When the colors become too pale, add more oil paint and turpentine mixture to the pan.

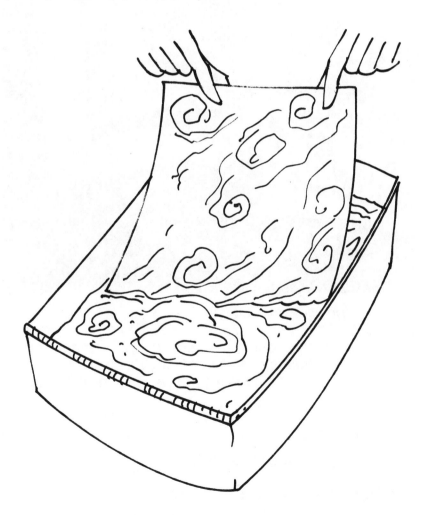

PHOTO COLLAGE PICTURE

Although we've specified two possible sizes for the base of this collage picture, you can make yours any size you'd like. The completed picture can be composed of a collection of photographs of just one family member or, as is shown here, several generations surrounding a family home. (A house is a good choice to give the picture unity.)

Tools and Materials

assorted family snapshots and photographs
scissors
illustration board, 10½ × 12½ or 5¼ × 7 inches
rubber cement
clear Lucite picture frame, in size to fit the piece of illustration board

Instructions

1. If you are making a small picture, you can cut out small heads, large heads, and full-length figures from existing snapshots or formal photographs and use a photo of a favorite scene for a background. Move the cutouts around on the piece of illustration board until you have a pleasing arrangement and then cement them in place. For a larger picture, choose the photos you wish to cut up and have separate, high-contrast photostats made of them, enlarging some and leaving others the same size. Cut out the pieces from the photostats and cement them in position.
3. Frame the picture in the Lucite frame.